FINDING COURAGE

THROUGH OUTDOOR ADVENTURES

FINDING COURAGE

THROUGH OUTDOOR ADVENTURES

KACHINA-CHALLENGE-REEVIS

GENE LEFEBVRE

Library of Congress Control Number: 2017919400
ISBN: Hardcover   978-1-5434-7449-7
                 Softcover   978-1-5434-7448-0
                 eBook   978-1-5434-7447-3

Print information available on the last page.

Cover Photo: David Radnich near Blue Lakes, San Juan Mountains, Colorado (Photo by Dale Childs, Kachina Archives)

Rev. date: 02/27/2018

To order additional copies of this book, contact:
Xlibris
1-888-795-4274
www.Xlibris.com
Orders@Xlibris.com
740781

Contents

Contents

Preface

This story began eighty years ago. Only sparse records were kept of parts of it. So, it seemed miraculous that we were able to gather as much of the story as you will see on these pages. We accessed articles and pictures from newspaper archives, and we found parts of two lost diaries. Student newspaper articles helped. Two people in Phoenix kept pictures and accounts in good order. It was a tribute to the power of the experiences that we heard in great detail in our interviews.

We know there are hundreds of memories of people who experienced the Kachinas, Pateman-Akin-Avery-Kachina (PAAK) Challenge, and Reevis Mountain School that we would love to hear. Kathy Pedrick will make her contribution as she completes her book, an expanded account of the early Kachinas. In addition, Kathy has arranged for the source material on the Kachinas and its heirs to reside in the Arizona Historical Society. It is also intriguing to think of sharing other stories yet only in our memories on social media.

Pinnacle Peak (Kachina Archives)

Lee Pedrick jumping across Pinnacle Peak, Scottsdale, Arizona (Kachina Archives)

Part One

The Kachinas

The Early Days

In 1949, I was sixteen and sitting in an auditorium at North Phoenix High School, mesmerized by what I saw on the screen. Boys who graduated from North High had returned to show us something that had been life changing for them. The film was professional in quality, and the subject was mountain climbing. They portrayed the fundamentals of climbing— belaying, climbing, and rappelling—against the background of nearby Camelback Mountain and Pinnacle Peak. Climbing— as they portrayed it—looked safe, exciting, and great fun. Sign me up.

I learned that they called themselves Kachina Mountaineers, and in 1947, they became a Senior Boy Scout troop in Phoenix. (Later, the title was changed to Explorer Post 1.) But they were unique among scout troops, for they focused on mountain climbing. They were, in fact, the first organized group of climbers in Arizona.

Kachinas are supernatural spirit beings that act as messengers between humans and the spirit world, according to the tradition of the Hopi Indians of northern Arizona. The boys called themselves Kachinas to honor the Hopi tradition and because they felt a call to the mountains where the kachinas dwelled.

Early Kachina emblem (Kachina Archives)

Ray Garner—photographer, explorer, and professional guide with Exum Petzoldt Climbing School at the Grand Teton National Park—had moved to Phoenix and molded this group of boys into an exceptional unit. The Camel's Head became their training ground, and they put up many routes, including Pedrick's Chimney, Hart Route, Ridge Route, Suicide, Pateman's Caves, and Praying Monk.

Dick Hart's first rappel (Kachina Archives)

2

Ben Pedrick became the leader among the boys. He was well organized, reliable, and skilled at climbing and had natural charisma. The boys learned well the rules of safe climbing and, under Ray's leadership, accomplished amazing feats. They made many of the first ascents in central Arizona. They climbed the highest volcanoes in Mexico, the notorious Lizard Head Peak in Colorado, Shiprock Mountain in New Mexico, and the Agathlan monolith in Monument Valley. Perhaps their greatest climb was to the peaks of the Teton Mountains in Wyoming. One year, they were the first climbers to go up the Tetons after the winter and spring snow.

Early Kachinas Ben Pedrick, Wynn Akin, Lee Pedrick, Roy Gray, Bob Owens, Ray Garner, Ed George in Saddle Mountains, east of Phoenix (Kachina Archives)

The Tetons, however, are also the site of the single greatest tragedy in their history. When Ben Pedrick and Wynn Akin climbed Nez Perce Peak in 1948—as they were enjoying the view from the top—a huge chunk of the peak broke off, hurling Wynn to his death.

Wynn Akin (Kachina Archives)

American alpine clubs thought it was an avoidable accident, saying they should have remained tied into safety lines while on the summit, even though they were standing several feet back from the edge. On that trip, they had traveled without any adults.

Grand Teton, Wyoming (Kachina Archives)

4

The Kachinas were not prone to fixing blame or letting tragedy defeat their love of climbing. But understandably, they experienced great grief, and their enthusiasm for the sport was never the same thereafter.

When measuring the accomplishments of the Kachinas, we must consider the great improvements that have been made in the sport since then. In those days, very few of us had boots designed for climbing. Some wore hiking boots; most wore tennis shoes. Today climbing shoes are much, much better. The ropes we used were nylon, not the superior ropes that have been designed specifically for climbing that we see now. Current ropes are made of the stronger Perlon material. There have also been large strides forward in the hardware used. And climbers now train both indoors and outdoors in a manner that we never could have imagined. Back then, should they get in trouble climbing, there was no one trained to rescue them. They had to rely on one another for rescue. Considering the changes that have taken place since then, some of the Kachina climbs were remarkable.

Belay and rappel off a spire in Eagletail Mountains, west of Phoenix (Kachina Archives)

Jim Waugh, well-known climber and historian of Arizona rock climbing, says, "Not enough can really be said about the Kachinas! Their pioneering spirit (then and now) has had tremendous impact on the history of climbing. Either directly or indirectly, their seed has spread to start other organizations."[1] We will write about this aspect of the Kachinas later in this book. These are the names I know of those early Kachinas: Ben and Lee Pedrick, Dick Hart, Ed George, Wynn Akin, Bob Owens, Jim Colburn, Bill McMorris, Roy Gray, and Ray Garner.

Early Kachinas (Kachina Archives)

Ray Garner taught climbing the old-fashioned way, and at the same time, it was unique for its era. The expansion

---

[1]   Jim Waugh, *Phoenix Rock: A Guide to Central Arizona Crags,* Phoenix: Polar Designs, 1987.

bolts he taught with were shorter than the bolts used by other climbers. This allowed bolts to be placed more quickly.

A rope and an anchor were used to catch a climber if he or she fell. They were also used for descent (rappel). But the climber could not use them or any mechanical device as an aid to climb up the mountain. Only when it was impossible to "climb free" was "artificial aid" allowed.

We knew that climbing groups like the Sierra Club used a rating system to determine the difficulty of a climb. But we did not. Why? Because it made climbing a competition that is distracting to the art. No rating climbs for us. Maybe we would have tried harder to complete a climb if it were rated. I think Ray had a nice balance between the science and the art of the sport. I know that some of my thoughts and feelings about climbing came from the art side. I came to see climbing as a kind of dance. It is also true that we had no standards by which we could rate a climb. Most of what we climbed in those days had never been climbed before. Imagine a whole state with first ascents ready for the taking.

I did not know Ray personally. I met him once, when he showed up at a presentation we were making. I barely knew Ben and Lee Pedrick either or the rest of that first generation of Kachinas. But I knew many of their stories, and I had great admiration for their climbing accomplishments and the men they became. Ray had instilled in them both safe-climbing guidelines and the joy of climbing in such a way that they could pass it on.

The Second Generation

Stan Lerch, Bob Radnich, Gerald Devore, and Gary Spencer joined the Kachinas at the same time I did. Our training began with easy routes on Camelback Mountain—Pedrick's Chimney and the Hart Route. These were perfect first climbs for us, easy but with exposure. They required a few different techniques: face climbing, chimney technique, belaying, and rappelling down. We were taught by boys who were more experienced than we were, ones who had passed the test of leading a series of climbs under the supervision of a rope leader. They, in turn, became rope leaders themselves. Ray and the early Kachinas were now gone.

John Goodson on Camelback Mountain practice rock
(Kachina Archives)

My third climb exposed me to a whole different level of climbing. The climb was called Suicide, which is a route on the largest cliff on Camelback. It must be five hundred feet high and much is overhang, that is, steeper than ninety degrees, requiring the climber to lean back from the cliff and defy the force of gravity. Ralph Pateman was the leader. He was my age but had already been in the Kachinas for a year. Ralph, Stan, and I climbed the first long section nicely, but then we came to the crux of the climb—a large protruding bump overhanging the wall. The route up was fixed with bolts that we could use.

Ralph attempted to bypass the overhang by circling to the right and over the top. He reached the overhang section, pounded in a piton with his left hand, and climbed back down to where I was belaying him. "I don't feel so great today. So, Gene, you try it," he said to me.

For god's sake, this was only my third climb, and I was scared to death, perched precariously a few hundred feet above the ground. But Ralph was our leader and trainer, so I followed his directions. I circled right and then up to the piton he'd tapped in, and then I hung there. It was on an overhang, and I couldn't find a handhold except the piton. I clipped my carabiner onto both the piton and my safety rope and then held on to the piton for a few more moments until it began to move. And then I fell. From my left, Ralph was belaying me, as well as Stan from fifty feet below.

I felt a momentary sense of relief as I let go, followed very quickly by a rush of fear. But the ropes caught me, and I hung dangling from the cliff about twenty feet below the piton.

Somehow the piton stayed in place; otherwise, I would have fallen an additional twenty feet.

Ralph shouted to me to climb back to where he sat, which I managed to do. He looked at me and said, "Gene, you still have a problem. Your rope is still clipped onto the piton. We can't go on until you climb to it, unclip your rope, and climb on."

Back across to the overhang and up to the piton with nothing to hang on to, I grabbed the piton; it moved again, and off I went into space. Again, the piton held. Damn it! Yes, it prevented me from falling that same twenty feet, but my problem remained. I went back up to Ralph. "Gene, you'll just have to climb back over there, unclip, and jump backward off the cliff."

Right. I felt totally exhausted, but there was no other choice. Once again, I climbed over to the piton. But this time, I unclipped, jumped off backward, and fell about thirty feet. Then I went back up to Ralph, who announced that we could now climb Suicide the way everyone else did. He led us up and over the bump, grabbing the bolts. Then Stan climbed, and finally, I followed. I was more than exhausted, but the last part of the route to the top was easy. We rested for only a few minutes on top, for darkness was on us. We scampered along the top of the cliff as darkness fell, and we damn near ran off the top of the monster cliff. We screeched to a halt just in time. I couldn't remember the rest of the hike down, only that we made it.

Suicide Cliff, largest cliff on Camelback Mountain—can you spot the climbers? (Kachina Archive)

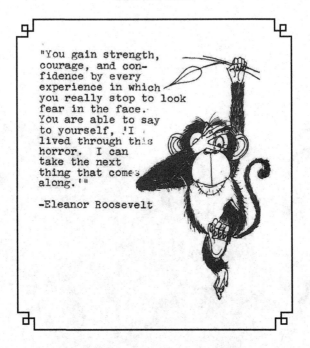

"You gain strength, courage, and confidence by every experience in which you really stop to look fear in the face. You are able to say to yourself, 'I lived through this horror. I can take the next thing that comes along.'"

-Eleanor Roosevelt

(PAAK Challenge Archives)

I had nightmares about that climb for at least a month. Still, I continued to finish my training. The rest of it seemed easy. I had survived, and the desire to climb hadn't been chased out of me. For the next year and a half, I enjoyed all the climbs—some more than others. No matter what, the fire still burned inside us, and we were having a good time.

Ralph Pateman, Stanford Lerch, Gene Lefebvre, Bob Radnich, Gerald Devore (North Phoenix High School, 1951, annual)

Let me tell you about Ralph Pateman. He was the quarterback for the North High football team and adept at many sports. He was one of the two best climbers among the Kachinas during my time. He seemed fearless and capable of intense concentration when he climbed. He also had a strange sense of humor, at times seeming to enjoy our discomfort, like when he would ask us to do a difficult climb. I guess I had passed one of his tests, though, by showing enough gumption to try a route up Suicide that hadn't yet been attempted.

Ralph was the kind of guy who decided to try bullfighting, so after graduating from North High, he arranged for instruction in nearby Nogales, Sonora, Mexico. He made his debut as a bullfighter in a Mexican bullring. It was a success, so he promptly quit and went on to other challenges. Ralph joined the marines and made that his career. Later, he died in a helicopter crash outside Marine Corps Air Station El Toro in California.

Most of us were pretty good athletes. Climbing was the best sport for some of us because it challenged us to overcome the fear of falling to our death. True, we were well trained to climb carefully, but there was always a chance that a rope or a piece of hardware might fail. And climbing established a trust unlike other activities; it became clear to us that our very lives depended on one another during the climbs.

Stan Lerch was a steady force among our group of friends. He was physically strong, emotionally tough, loyal, and dependable, and he easily made lots of friends. He also enjoyed life in school and hanging out with his buddies. He could argue about most any subject, and none of us were surprised when he chose law as his profession.

One night on the way to a church basketball game, Stan got in my car. There were three passengers already in the back. Stan looked in the back seat and said, "Who the hell is that back there? I can't make out your —— face." It was my mother. Eventually, my mother and Stan got over it, but that story has been repeated more than any other from our high school years.

Bob Radnich (Kachina Archives)

Bob Radnich moved to Phoenix around the time he entered high school. He said the Kachinas gave him a great opportunity to learn a new skill that was both thrilling and fun, along with the chance to become close with his fellow climbers. He soon learned the sport well enough to become an instructor, which he enjoyed immensely, and it was a kick to take girls along when we felt free to do so. The Kachinas gave Bob a sense of belonging, a sense of competence at a challenging sport, and recognition for his ability to teach others something about which he was passionate.

The body of Bob's father was ravaged with arthritis. Bob and his mother spent a lot of time taking care of him. One of Bob's ways of dealing with that tragedy was to occasionally make fun of the situation. I think only high-school-aged boys understand that kind of dark humor.

Bob was a joy to have along on a climb. He also had a sense of light humor and was a great laugh. It was clear to the rest of us that he loved being in the mountains. He believed, to his last days, that the Kachina experience was a great, positive force with regard to shaping his life and future.

In a sense, we were an odd lot to our peers. No one else was into being in an organized group of climbers. In fact, it was a sport barely known in Arizona. Then why were so many of us attracted to it, especially with the whirl of other social activities and sports? It was hard to explain. Sometimes we would quote George Mallory, a famous Mount Everest climber, saying, "We climb it because it is there."

Many years later, I learned that, in our culture, we separate the animate from the inanimate like we do living things from nonliving things. We learn not to express feelings toward inanimate objects. It's no wonder we couldn't find the words to explain what it was about climbing that turned us on. Feelings of excitement, fear, frustration, and accomplishment were common and easy to express. As young men, though, it was difficult to express the love we felt for one another. And the feeling of harmony with the mountains, beauty, trust in creation, and such were also rarely, if ever, spoken of.

Author in a chimney at Granite Mountain, Prescott (PAAK Challenge Archives)

We were always careful to practice safety. We had to pay attention to what we were doing on the mountain more so than other moments in our teenage lives. We had close calls while driving—ones that were more dangerous than most of our escapades on the rocks. But I can only remember one serious climbing accident during those years. We were climbing the easy Hart Route on Camelback when a rock fell and hit one of our companions on his head, creating a large gash. It knocked him off his feet, and he fell a few feet down the cliff, far enough to break his leg. We evacuated him to the hospital, where it took him several weeks to recover. Considering we had no adult supervision on our adventures, we had an impressive safety record.

John Goodson joined the Kachinas during a time of transition; the original Kachinas were leaving. Only Lee Pedrick was around to teach climbing skills to John and a few others who had recently joined. By the time my friends and I joined, John was already off to college. He enjoyed climbing, but he wasn't finished with his dream of mountaineering. He built his life around what Joseph Campbell called "the myth of the hero's journey." This is the life story of a person who leaves home, conquers many obstacles, finds the great treasure (the meaning of his life), and returns home to share his hard-earned wisdom. In John's mind, the first part of that journey was a great adventure where he would lead a group of brave comrades to a successful goal and return home feeling stronger and wiser.

John struck people in different ways. Some saw him as strange and others as a force of nature, but everyone thought he was unique. He was physically strong, intense (too intense for some), bursting with ideas, and full of energy and determination. He was smart and generous with his friends. Unless he was leading an expedition, he preferred to lead from the side. What I mean is that rather than running for president of an organization, he'd prefer to take another role in which he could cause things to happen—without being bothered with the responsibility of the traditional role of "the leader." While a student at the University of Arizona, he decided it would be fun to get someone unknown elected to be the president of the school's student body. He selected a fraternity brother who was virtually unknown, a recent transfer from Ohio State, but John was confident in the campaign and succeeded. His victory is still remembered by many alumni.

John Goodson with camera, 1951 (Kachina Archives)

The Baja, Mexico, Expedition

John dreamed up an adventure and recruited five comrades to climb the highest mountain in Baja California—La Encantada. He had read that four or five attempts on this peak had failed, but he believed that, under his leadership, we would conquer it. Off we went in August of 1950—six brave, determined, and naive boys packed into the Kachina vehicle, which was a 1937 army ambulance. The ambulance was a monster four-wheel-drive truck with dual rear wheels. It had a small space for the driver, the navigator, a large load of gear, and four uncomfortable boys.

The trip took ten days, eight days of hiking plus two for traveling from Phoenix to the trailhead and back. La Encantada rose to the top of the San Pedro Mártir mountains, located in the center of Baja between the Pacific Ocean and the Sea of Cortez, south of Ensenada, the capital city of Baja.

Kachina transportation—retired army ambulance (Kachina Archives)

The paved highway turned to dirt south of Ensenada. That dirt road became rougher and rougher, and the dust became so thick that Stan Lerch had to sit on the front fender and signal directions. I stood on the running board and relayed Stan's directions to Gerald Devore, the driver. Bob Radnich, Gary Spencer, and John Goodson all stood on the back bumper, trying to keep the roof rack from flying off.

In the late afternoon, we arrived at our destination, San José, which consisted of one large ranch house, corrals, and many small buildings. And about fifty vaqueros (cowboys) were hanging out in the town square and staring fiercely at us. Well, it was no wonder they stared with four of us still hanging off the truck and all of us covered in dirt and dust. We decided the direct approach was best, so we trooped over to the center of the group of men and asked (in Spanish) where to find Mr.

and Mrs. Millings, our contacts here. They asked us questions about who we were and where we were going until we ran out of our meager Spanish vocabulary.

At that point, an older man spoke in clear English. "If you aim to climb La Encantada, you're in for a hell of a journey." It was Mr. Millings. He had been testing our Spanish before switching to English. He invited us to camp across the stream, and he said he'd call for us when supper was ready. "We're going to feed this whole bunch," he said, pointing to the men around us. "So a few more people, that's no problem."

The Millingses were a godsend. We had only a crude map and a vague idea of how to get to the mountain. Their description of the road that would take us from San José to the trailhead would at least get us started in the right direction. After supper, Gerald went back to work on nursing the truck engine for the next day's journey, and then we got a good night's sleep.

The road was extremely rough past San José, and our poor ambulance barely made it to the trailhead. The trail emerged through chaparral growth and went higher than we expected. It wasn't long until we found ourselves in very large trees. That first day was very tough. We had inadequate packs in which we had stuffed our gear, making them weigh a ton—well, more than fifty pounds each. The path forward was steep, and the heat was oppressive. We were not ready to begin hiking until the afternoon, and our directions said that it would be eight miles before we came to a stream. It seemed we might have to camp without water that night. We hiked until we were exhausted, well after dark.

Just when we were ready to give up, we smelled food cooking and came upon a small group of vaqueros camping out by a stream and cooking dinner. We camped nearby and were then able to ask the same question we asked everyone we came across from there on. "What is the name of this place, and how far is it to the next water?"

We struggled on, now with blistered feet, for another two days. That night, we became well aware of the altitude we gained, for we almost froze in our thin sleeping bags. Actually, Stan and Bob managed better than the rest of us—at first. They decided, after a couple of hours of the cold, to climb into one sleeping bag together. From then on, we paired up every night—which also had the added benefit of letting us lighten our load by stashing three of the sleeping bags, which we would pick up on our way back down. We left behind anything that wasn't absolutely needed.

John Goodson with eighty-pound pack (Kachina Archives)

Stan, John, and Bob were the three strongest hikers, and they decided to carry the heaviest loads. They also decided they wanted my pack to be manageable because they felt that I was the best climber. They needed me to lead the difficult climb up La Encantada once we reached the peak. I wasn't convinced I was the best climber, but considering the title came with a lighter pack, I humbly agreed. Bob proved to be the best scout when we were looking for the trail, often a difficult task.

Author, exhausted on Baja trip, 1950 (Kachina Archives)

In the morning of the fifth day, our fatigue showed itself in an argument about who should be the first one to leave their warm sleeping bag to start a fire that would enable us to cook breakfast. That argument repeated itself every morning for the rest of the hike. I knew from his journal that John felt a heavy responsibility for the success of the trip and that the arguing gnawed at him. The older Kachinas had first thought of this expedition, and when it became apparent they'd all be gone before it was enacted, they asked John to lead it. John hadn't "just dreamed up this trip" as we thought; instead, he'd been commissioned to lead it by the original members. John agreed and worked terrifically hard to make it happen. He believed that it had to succeed. If it didn't, not only would he feel it as a failure of his leadership ability but the Kachinas also would probably end as an organization. The success of this trip would carry the Kachinas through the transition to the next phase of its life. It had to work. So John sometimes "carried the group on his back" by urging us onward and by his example of absolute determination to reach our goal.

At one point, Stan tried to encourage John and the rest of us when he said, "My god, John, we are trying to accomplish something that four or five expeditions failed to do—climb La Encantada. And they had to have been a hell of a lot better equipped." Stan made a good point. We had lousy packs and sleeping bags, inadequate food (we felt like we were starving most of the time), no real maps, and barely enough water. We were banking on our willpower, some skill, and a lot of luck.

We saw glimpses of the peak that day, but try as we might, we could not find a trail that led in that direction. After a few hours, we unanimously agreed that there was no such a trail. John, Bob, and Stan agreed to scout directly cross-country until they made it to the base of the peak. They dropped their packs, and then wearing only shoes, Levi's shorts, and T-shirts, they took off at a fast pace. They climbed about two thousand feet through huge boulder fields encircled with dense undergrowth. Finally, the land flattened out, and they came to a meadow. They searched all through and around the meadow, looking for water, but there was none. Rain clouds were closing in, and the sun was sinking behind the mountains. Our scouting party gave up.

When the rain turned into hail, Bob shouted, "Oh god, we'll really be commandos if we get out of this!" The three of them began to run fast to keep warm and stay ahead of the hailstorm. They yelled as they dodged undergrowth and bolted around and over the boulders. Down they ran as the wash they were following continued to narrow. They knew that the wash would fill with runoff water soon—there were steep drops in the wash that would soon become waterfalls. At the bottom of the drops were sandy bottoms. When they came to the first fall, they jumped down into the sand, screaming as they went. They felt great and continued lumbering down the wash. When a fall was too great, they slid down the sides of the wet boulders instead. They felt nothing could stop them.

When they reached flat ground, they looked at one another. "We were just initiated into the commandos." They agreed to start a group within the Kachinas called the Commandos, who would be ready for the hardest challenges. Other members of the Kachinas would also be inducted as Commandos, infusing the spirit into the whole group.

The next morning, we threw the rest of the food in to a pot and cooked "cream-o-scotch," butterscotch pudding mixed with Cream of Wheat. It was awful, but that was all we had. Once again, we stashed everything—to be picked up on the way back—and left with only our climbing gear, a canteen of water each, and the movie camera to hike toward the peak.

Climbing a crevasse in Baja California (Kachina Archives)

We saw the three peaks that the Millingses told us would hide our view of La Encantada. We struggled up a canyon between the second and third peaks. From the saddle, we could see a huge, half-mile-wide gorge. The Millingses had also told us we would find this monster gorge called El Diablo (the devil) between ourselves and our goal. The gorge wandered down ten thousand feet to the desert floor and beyond to the Sea of Cortez.

We decided to traverse across and down the canyon about one thousand feet to a spot where we could climb the cliffs on the other side. We scrambled laterally down and across the rocky terrain by clinging to vegetation as we walked along narrow ledges made by the round surfaces and cracks in the boulders. Then we came to a gully that went about a mile to the rock climb of the next peak. We bulled our way up this for the next two hours, thinking we would be glad once we got to the some "real" rock climbing. We felt jubilant when we reached the cliffs. There were cracks in the granite too wide for pitons but wide enough to jam a foot, arm, or hand in to climb up. Stan and I traded off leading the group, stopping often to belay one another up with a rope.

By 2:00 p.m., we had reached the summit. There was no sign that anyone else had ever made this climb, which made us feel good, but our joy was short-lived. The two higher peaks, which the day before had appeared to be a few hundred yards of easy climbing compared with the one we were now on, were really across another gorge as deep as El Diablo. What we had seen the day before was an optical illusion. We looked down, way down into the gorge beneath us. Once again, the mountains had fooled us.

Summit of the second highest peak in Baja (Kachina Archives)

"Shall we try the other peak?" John asked. We all looked long and hard at the scene. Finally, Stan said he was up for it if the rest of us were. I said it would be a tough long hike down and back up the second peak, including a long cliff climb. I didn't think we had the equipment to do it. We would need expansion bolts to safely climb the steepest cliffs, and we hadn't brought any with us. Bob said he didn't want to tell people back home that we had chickened out. Gerry said it was going to be hard enough just to climb back to where we started. He thought we could just tell people we had climbed the peak—no one else would ever come this way. I was getting angry, telling them that we didn't want to live with a lie.

John had his heart set on climbing the peak not only for personal accomplishment but also for the sake of the future of the Kachinas. I later saw in his notes how he weighed everything in his mind, and the deciding factor for him was safety. Our only food was back at camp, and there was very little water between here and there. What would happen if even one of us couldn't make it back to camp because of injury or exhaustion? The sun would set soon, and we would be going back in the dark. This place was so isolated that there was virtually no chance of rescue. Hell, we would be lucky if we could just get our whole group back across El Diablo safely. And John trusted my assessment of the difficult climbing obstacles.

"Well," he said to us, "we climbed the second highest peak in Baja, and we proved we could do more than any of us had ever thought we could in these conditions. Time to retreat until another day." We knew how invested John was in this effort, so none of us questioned his judgment. We turned back, deflated and relieved at the same time.

We found that the water in the rock potholes had mostly dried up on our trip back to camp, making it a long, hard struggle. As a diversion, we talked about food—what Mexican food we could buy in San José, if we could we find a restaurant that would prepare steak for us in Ensenada, the best place to get a hamburger in San Diego, what favorite foods we wanted when we got home, etc.

We made it home a little beat up, proud that we survived, and only a little wiser. The Baja expedition led to an even riskier adventure the following summer.

The Expedition into the Sierra Madre
Mountains of Mexico, August 1951

We were standing in the yard of his ranch—six young men from Phoenix, ages eighteen to twenty-two. Mr. Montgomery was a Mexican rancher who emigrated from Germany many years ago and now owned a ranch here in Mexico. We were in his yard because John Goodson, our trip leader nicknamed Commando, had seen a *Life* magazine article describing an expedition to a canyon in the Sierra Madres that was deeper than the Grand Canyon. The writer described their trip to the Barrancas del Cobre as the first by any outsiders. The expedition encountered many hardships in their journey: mountains and rivers to cross, rugged hiking for hundreds of miles, and native Tarahumara Indians who hid from strangers and posed a serious threat to those who might come to do them harm. John was inspired by the article and decided he could put together an expedition to follow in the footsteps of those explorers.

We found the tiny town of Guiracoba on August 7, 1951. It was the jump-off point for the *Life* expedition. It was forty kilometers from Alamos, an old silver-mining town hundreds of miles south of the Arizona border. John described our interest in becoming the second outside group to explore the canyon to Mr. Montgomery. We knew the old rancher had recruited a guide for the *Life* expedition, so we asked if he would help us too.

The rancher looked us over with skeptical eyes. The *Life* expedition had first-class equipment, several experienced explorers, and the money to afford whatever they needed. In contrast, we were six inexperienced young boys with meager resources and second-class gear at best.

But after pausing to think it over, he said, "Well, I'll give you this. You certainly are full of piss and vinegar." Chuck Register, the oldest and wisest of our group, had to explain to us that this was an old-fashioned expression to describe the adventurous but often foolhardy attitude of youth. We were to discover just how full of piss and vinegar we were—or not. Here we were— John Goodson, photographer and translator; Stan Lerch, camp cook and historian; Blake Wallace, camp organizer; Chuck Register, mechanic and the wise man of our group; Brice Dille, medic; and me, Gene Lefebvre, navigator and lead climber.

The rancher introduced us to Juan, the Mexican man who guided the *Life* magazine party. After lengthy negotiations, he agreed to guide us. We would also need a mule, two burros, and a mule skinner, so he recruited the animals and a fellow named Manuel for the trip. Thankfully, we had enough money in our budget. We put our trust in the guide, for we had no maps of the area and no devices by which to determine where we were on the face of the earth.

When we left the ranch the next day, we made a parade of two donkeys, a mule, two Mexican guides, and six crazy gringos. Oh yes, there was an important warning the guide had for us before we left: this was August, the rainy season. Our trip would be more difficult than the one our predecessors had experienced. We would have to climb higher mountain ridges because of rain runoff. And when we couldn't climb high enough, we might have to swim across rivers. Great, even more adventure.

Type of mule used on Barranca trip, along with burros
(Dale A. Childs)

Each of us carried a heavy pack filled with climbing gear and camera equipment. We thought the canyon would be composed of steep cliffs, and John had convinced certain influential people that we would bring back a film of Mexico's Grand Canyon to show at the Arizona State Fair. Of course, we also carried camping gear, clothes, medical supplies, cooking gear, food, and so on. Our packs weighed about sixty to seventy pounds each. Since I was the navigator, I took graph paper and drew a line each day to represent our trail, using a compass for directions. We had found no maps of the area, and we certainly did not have a sextant, much less a GPS. At the end of each day, I asked the other five people how far they thought we had hiked. I took the average and reduced it by about one-third—probably the easiest and least accurate form of land navigation.

The following day-by-day account is based on my memory, supported by Stan and John's recollections. At the end of the trip, when we hiked back to the trailhead, there were some days about which we had no memory at all. As you read the account, the reason will become clear.

August 8, 1951: On our first hiking day, we were ready for a hearty breakfast of Roman ration. Stan and John had raved about it after their taste trial at home. They must have been drunk when they tested it. It was awful. We had brought one hundred pounds of the stuff and counted on it as our main source of nourishment. Brice suggested we keep an eye on our guides, lest they slip back home to get some decent food. I don't know about the guides, but I was ready to go back home for real food, and by the look of my companions, the feeling was unanimous. But there was no turning back—we were totally committed to our adventure.

The trail entered a jungle right away. Juan was working hard, hacking away vines with his machete. All morning, we crossed and recrossed a river heading downstream. For lunch, we ate cheese, and then we went back on the trail, hiking hard the rest of the day, talking about how crazy we were to begin this adventure and how there was a message we had for the nutritionist back in Phoenix who had so glorified the benefits of the Roman ration. Juan and Manuel ate with the local natives and then came by for a courtesy cup of wheat. We fed the leftovers to the chickens. We traded some of our wheat to the natives for corn tortillas.

We spent the night in a leaky lean-to. We stuffed our sleeping bags into plastic tubes, which worked to keep out the rain but also kept air from circulating over the bags. We were soon quite wet in our Mickey Mouse shelters as we now called them. Our situation was so bad that we made up things that could possibly have made it worse.

Barranca del Cobre, Chihuahua, Mexico (Kachina Archives)

August 9: Seventeen miles didn't sound far for a day's hike, but part of it was up a very steep hill. The clouds hung low, and the air was sticky with humidity. John, burdened down with camera equipment, was having a tough time. Unfortunately, Stan picked this moment to say something snarky to John, who proceeded to chase him down the mountain until he got control of his anger. I thought we were reaching our limit, but no, more was to come.

But this day was to end on a positive note. When we reached the top of the hill, we could see the trail wandering into a pretty valley. Down below in the town of Gusto, we found a store where we were able to buy some sugar. We took shelter in their storehouse for the night.

August 10: This morning we found that one of the burros had rolled over during the night and broken our supplies, including our medicine for dysentery. We knew it was critical, but all we could do was pray for healthy bodies. Brice seemed to enjoy too much tending to our blisters. He would grab an offending foot, pour on the Merthiolate, and smile while we yelled.

We hiked another seventeen miles today to the town of Descanso. We spent the evening fighting gnats. They were everywhere, including in our soup, and they were legion. As Stan put it, "Only hope is prodding us on." In our case, it was the hope of reaching the cool pine forests Juan had promised were ahead.

August 11: We awoke early, driven out of our sleeping bags by fleas—at least a thousand fleas. We had to sit around half the day waiting for the opportunity to cross the Chiapas River by ferry, a little boat with two men at oars and many leaks. After each trip, the ferrymen had to bail out the boat. It took five ferry trips and fifteen pesos for each trip, about $1.50 each. We spent a lot of time impatiently waiting until we could get everything across. We passed the night in a hut with fifteen other people, as well as pigs, dogs, chickens, goats, and one cat.

Juan was popular wherever we went. Younger people called him *tio* (uncle). A circle of children surrounded him each night until bedtime.

Crossing terrain in the Barranca (Philip A. Robbins).

August 12: We rose before dawn and had a good meal of beans and tortillas. We hiked until late afternoon when we finally reached pine trees. From the top of a ridge, we could see the countryside ahead. The rainy season had made everything green, and we could see the deep canyons and high ridges with valleys in between.

We were happy as we hiked along that day and started singing camp songs. We spent the night in a small cabin and went to sleep with the sound of tropical rain in our ears, a rain that was now with us every evening.

August 13: A trail that had been very rocky turned to sticky mud by the overnight rain. It ran up from a little canyon toward a deep one. At one point, we passed a grave. Juan told us the tradition of placing a little coin by the marker for good luck. We followed the tradition.

There was another rain that evening, and our only shelter was one tarp, which we strung between the limbs of two trees—all of us huddled together with the equipment around us.

August 14: We named a valley we entered that day "the Valley of the Vampire Fleas," insects that looked like fleas but were much smaller. They swarmed all over us overnight, sucking blood until they were too full to fly.

Author overlooking the Barranca del Cobre (Kachina Archives)

Today's climb took us out of the valley. We tried to hurry the animals to cut down on our hiking time. But hurrying burros proved to be impossible.

Chuck kept falling behind the group. Dr. Brice said Chuck had dysentery, and of course, it was the dysentery medicine that had been broken and drained out when the burro rolled over. We were absolutely famished by the time we stopped for lunch. We were so hungry that we were glad that Chuck was too sick to eat his share.

A couple of hours after lunch, Juan told us we would have to stop for the evening. He pointed to a cabin up ahead and said there were no more shelters on the trail for a long time. In the cabin, we had a good change of diet. For a set of earrings produced by Stan, we obtained all the potatoes, tomatoes, and peppers we could eat. It was a good meal, and we appreciated the shelter from the rain. We decided the Barranca hike wasn't so bad after all.

August 15: This morning I announced to the group how the Romans had conquered Gaul. They were so fed up with their wheat that they crossed the Alps and conquered Gaul for a change of diet. After two cups of Roman rations, I noticed some of the group eyeing the chickens running around the cabin with evil thoughts in their minds.

Tarahumara home (Philip A. Robbins)

Tarahumara family (Philip A. Robbins)

Juan told us that he preferred the low trail to the canyon, but it was blocked because of the rain. He said we'd be the first group to try to reach the canyon by the high trail. Our trail took us across a flat valley, and we started singing as we enjoyed the easy hike.

Before sunset, we saw a large hacienda made of stone and surrounded by fields of corn and corrals full of cattle, horses, and goats. It looked beautiful. The rancher was gracious and conveyed an easy hospitality. He gave us milk, tortillas, and apples—all the green apples we could eat. We weren't hungry that night, but we all suffered indigestion from too many apples.

August 16: Chuck was so sick that he did not carry anything today, and we split his load among us. Juan had been gathering leaves from along the trail. He made a tea and fed it to Chuck. From the look on Chuck's face, it was an obnoxiously bitter drink, but he managed to drink it all. Juan told us we could save two days by leaving the pack animals and Manuel here at the hacienda. The trail from here was too steep for the animals anyway, and it would save us time. We agreed and decided to leave behind our sleeping bags too and bring along one blanket apiece. We also left behind anything else that wasn't essential.

Juan hired a young Indian boy to show us the trail, and we proceeded to pack our food, camera gear, climbing gear, and blankets. The Indian boy took Chuck's share and rolled it in a pack made of a little blanket and then threw it across his shoulders. Chuck was very weak. We quickly learned that our young guide was very strong. He almost ran the downhill sections and climbed the uphill sections fast and easy.

Somehow Chuck made it up the ridge. Finally, we were at the crest of the trail at about ten thousand feet high. It was the hardest hike any of us had ever made. Our young guide left us to return home with our greatest gratitude. We settled down for the night, again sleeping in a small cabin. With only one blanket each, we were very cold. We decided to share blankets, three of us sleeping together. Still, we got hardly any sleep.

August 17: We woke up cold but in sight of a roaring fire outside the cabin door. Blake had risen early and built the fire. It warmed not only our bodies but also our spirits.

Our greatest worry was Chuck. The cold nights were very hard on him. How in the world could he make it into and out of the canyon?

We followed a creek downhill until it turned into a beautiful waterfall. It was there we got our first glimpse of the canyon. After months of preparation and this extremely difficult hike, we had finally arrived.

Waterfall in the Barranca del Cobre
(Copper Canyon) (Kachina Archives)

As we walked down the trail, we could see the difference between the Barrancas del Cobre and the Grand Canyon of Arizona. The Grand Canyon has steep vertical walls of many colors; the Barranca walls are not so steep and covered with vegetation, so one could not see the rock colors, only shades of green, nor could we see peaks and plateaus rising inside as we would in the Grand Canyon. But this was a huge deep, hidden canyon with a beauty all of its own.

After seeing this much of the canyon, Chuck decided he could not make it down and back. Brice decided it was his role as trip doctor to stay with Chuck. We all knew how this decision was for both Brice and Chuck. So we left them with some food, knowing we would be gone for at least a full day.

We did not encounter cliffs to rappel from or climb down, for there were none, only a trail that was quite negotiable. We'd carried ropes and heavy pitons and carabiners for nothing. By evening, we had reached the bottom of the canyon, and we could see the village of Urique ahead. We felt strong, proud, and humble as we set out for the village. We walked down a dirt street between deserted buildings. A few kids and old people watched us march into Urique. Two men, who identified themselves as the mayor and the chief of police of Urique, came over to greet us and invited us to stay at the abandoned brewery house.

Almost all the buildings were obviously empty. We did find one little store open. It carried the one thing we desired: animal crackers. We bought ten pounds of animal crackers that had come from Chihuahua. We shared some with the children and enjoyed eating the rest.

August 18: After a night sleeping in the brewery, we woke up tired and stiff. We'd promised donors we would bring back a film of the trip to show at the Arizona State Fair coming up in November. We had just a few hours to take shots of Urique and of the canyon from below.

The mayor showed us around, and we began to see the town's history as a little silver-mining town. The ore machines were fascinating. They were placed in the water on the edge of the river. A circular wooden frame and paddles on long arms would turn by the river flow and crush rock to separate out the silver ore. We could imagine the burros carrying raw material into the village and taking ore out along those very steep trails.

All of us had worn boots going into the hike. By now, all were worn out. Most of us had backup Keds from gym class. We threw our boots away on the way out and found the Keds to work better on the uneven terrain. Two of our hikers made different choices. Blake contracted with one of the Indians to make him a pair of native sandals, which he accomplished within a few hours. He found them to be very satisfactory. Stan just made do with his old boots, which were a constant nuisance to him.

The hike out of the canyon was torture, but we were starting home, so we would endure. We appreciated the beautiful views of the canyon.

We found Chuck and Brice waiting for us at a creek crossing. They had suffered an awful night, crouching under an overhang, trying to avoid a torrential rain. They had become completely drenched and were cursing a lot. That night had been hard, but miraculously, Chuck was free from dysentery.

Juan led us back to the cabin on top of the rim. We chose to spend the night huddled around the campfire instead of trying to sleep as we still carried just one blanket each.

August 19: Three of us, including me, refused to eat the wheat the next morning, and we gave the remainder to the Indians. We were through with Roman ration forever. We had some beans and tortillas but not enough. We were starving. It was a difficult hike down the ridge, especially for Stan with his dilapidated boots. Chuck was doing well, but Blake had to stop frequently.

Waterfall in the Barranca (Kachina Archives)

We welcomed the site of the big hacienda. The family celebrated our return by inviting us to eat with them. The meal looked great with fresh tortillas and beans and large bowls of soup. But oh no, the soup was made from wheat swimming in goat's milk. They had seen us eating it on the way in and thought it was a delicacy of ours. We <u>had</u> to eat it and then had little appetite for anything else.

August 20: Blake made many trips into the cornfield that night. John and I were also sick to our stomachs. Juan's mule sensed home and took off during the night. It was the last we saw of her until the end of the trip.

August 21–23: Our notes were lost for these days. It doesn't matter really; none of us could remember what happened. We had just kept hiking along in a daze.

August 24: Hiking was okay this day—but our minds were more in blur. Somehow about that time in the trip, we became paranoid about Juan's leadership. I don't know what triggered it, but it did bloom in our minds. We came to think he was lying to us and leading us in circles—or at least in the wrong direction—and keeping us going so he could demand more money when we finally arrived at our vehicle. I don't think Juan did anything to encourage this paranoia, but it was very strong.

Blake still looked like the victim of a refugee camp—extremely thin with ribs plainly showing.

August 25: After the trip, Stan told me this day had been his birthday. He didn't say a word about it at the time. He felt there was no emotional energy for a birthday celebration.

We crossed a big river by ferry again, taking several trips across throughout the day. But we did make it to Descanso. Juan told us we would make it back to Guiracoba the next day. This was great news, but we lacked the energy even to celebrate that.

August 26: The twenty-eight-mile hike to Guiracoba was, no surprise, exhausting. We hiked through flooded washes and the deep Agua Caliente River. Stan found the energy to start us singing again during the last five miles. We all but ran the final mile. Here, we found ourselves again at the Guiracoba ranch.

We took the time to eat and then crawled into our sleeping bags and fell into a deep sleep.

August 27: The next morning, we experienced celebration and joy. We had made it back to the ranch, our starting point. All our bad thoughts about Juan were gone, and we thanked him effusively. We even gave him a bonus. All the people at the ranch were glad we were back. Mr. Montgomery was surprised to see us. He had thought it would take us another ten days to complete the journey, so he was impressed.

We bathed, ate good food, rested, and laughed for the first time in several days. Mr. Montgomery regaled us with stories of Pancho Villa's visit to the ranch years earlier with his small army on their way to the revolution.

Then we were ready to load up and leave for home. But the damn truck wouldn't start. Chuck fooled with the wiring, and we pushed the truck down the dirt road, trying to start it. One time we hooked it up to mules and had them pull it. Still, we could not get it started. It was so disheartening.

We decided that we would have to take the truck battery back to Alamos to have it charged or replaced. We had no transportation, so we decided to draw straws to see who would hike back the twenty-four miles to Alamos to get the job done. I drew the short straw and went into shock at the thought of hiking that distance, carrying the battery. Stan saw the look on my face and volunteered to go with me. Bless him. With his offer, I thought we could make it.

We decided to try one more time. Darned if the truck didn't start. We loaded our stuff and took off, waving to the folks at the ranch.

We stopped at Alamos again on our way from Guiracoba. John's connections there included a family who let us stay with them on the way in and again that night. They fed us a simple meal, and we slept. A photo was taken of us in Alamos. Our skin was darkened by the sun, we wore beards, and we all were skinny. Chuck had lost over twenty pounds, the rest of us at least ten pounds each.

We made contact in Alamos with the chief of police, another of John's connections. He too was surprised to see us. We told him we tried to see him on the way in, but he had been at his birthday party. He laughed and said he had several birthdays a year. Then he told us in a very serious voice that had he seen us on the way in, he would have done everything in his power to stop us. The people of Alamos had many stories about the dangers of the trip we had taken—stories of natives who hid behind trees with bows and arrows and attacked strangers, stories of alligators at the bottom of the river deep in the canyon, and more such stories until we were laughing heartily. "Stop laughing," he said. "This is serious. We've heard many stories and believe some of them are true. And yet here you are, safe in Alamos. *Gracias a Dios.*"

August 28: We had a really good meal in a restaurant in Navojoa. After half an hour or so, Chuck noticed that the many filled tables had emptied out while we sat there. He told us to shut up and listen to him. He realized our terrible language had driven people away. Being alone in the wild where we were the only ones who spoke English, we had developed some very bad habits of speaking gross language. As soon as we realized we were offending people, we quickly finished eating, paid our bill, and left.

We were traveling through the streets of Navojoa when a local cop waved us down and escorted us to the police station. He had seen us traveling too fast down the street, so he ran down an alley and caught us at the next intersection. We stood before two officers in the local police office and pleaded our case. We were poor young men who had no money and were unable to pay a fine. We had clear evidence on our side: we looked emaciated, we were dressed in ragged clothes, and there were only a couple of dollars in our collective pockets. Well, okay, we had hidden some of our money under equipment before getting out of the truck, but we seemed pathetic. I know this was so because the police told us to go home and get cleaned up. They must have felt so sorry for us that they dismissed the fine.

We drove day and night to get to Arizona. Six sick boys crossed the border at Nogales, and six exhausted boys sacked out at the Phi Delta Theta Fraternity House in Tucson, to which Chuck, John, and Stan belonged. It was five o'clock in the morning of August 29, 1951. After several hours of sleep, we traveled home to Phoenix.

Our folks were thrilled to see us and very glad to find us safe. That first week home, we ate far too much rich food, and our digestive systems suffered outrage. Doctors determined that Chuck, Blake, and Brice were suffering from malaria, and two of them also had contracted amoebic dysentery. After a while, we all recovered. In November, we told our story to hundreds of people in a booth at the Arizona State Fair, where we showed a half-hour film that John had edited.

We did learn about Maslow's hierarchy of needs on our trip. After a couple of days in, I couldn't remember any of our conversations being about sex or sports. Imagine six young men going for many days without talk about two of our favorite topics. Maybe it's just that I can't remember those talks, but I remember very clearly our conversations and dreams about cool, clear water and about food—all kinds of food, huge amounts of our favorite foods—and about comfortable beds in dry rooms. It is also true that I don't remember feeling fearful at any point on the trip—exhausted, sick, almost ready to quit, yes, but not afraid.

We also learned about our limits. Repeatedly, we felt as if we had reached our physical limit, but somehow we kept going, even when we were so sick that we couldn't carry our share of the load. Over the course of blocking out the agony from some of those days, we had also blocked out the memories of several *whole* days. After years of coming to terms that those memories might be forgotten forever, finding the lost journals of John and Stan was a real gift.

The expedition greatly affected each of us. We learned a lot and (at least for a while) depleted our supply of piss and vinegar. It may sound as though a couple of more days would have led to violence among us, considering our physical and emotional condition. But I don't think so. First, I don't recall anything close to a fight brewing. Second, John, Stan, and I had deep bonds with one another that grew out of our climbing experience and the Commando Baja expedition. I suspect our relationship helped keep things from falling apart. As an aside, I wonder if it was just a coincidence that the three of us didn't contract malaria or amoebic dysentery.

Forty-five years later, I returned to the Barrancas del Cobre with a group from my church. This time, we traveled on an impressive railroad that had been built in the 1960s. We stayed at a lodge close to the canyon and had the opportunity to see it from rim vistas, even from the windows of a small plane. In preparation for this trip, we studied about the Tarahumara people. We learned that they had resisted acculturation by Spanish and Mexican peoples for hundreds of years. According to one anthropologist, out of all the populations living in the Americas, they remain the most similar to the way they had lived ages ago. By now, they had become world famous for their long-distance running. We had the chance to meet some of these people and witness some of their native religious dances. And yes, there was a young man similar to that sixteen-year-old boy who had guided us to the canyon.

We did not fully appreciate how important these Mexico expeditions were in lessening our fear. It helped teach us about respecting a culture foreign to us and its people of another language.

Second Teton Expedition

While some of us were absorbed with the Barranca expedition, unknown to us, Gary Driggs pulled together a second climbing trip to the Teton Mountains in Wyoming. Drawing from the ranks of younger Kachinas, he formed a strong team that included him, Danny Kleinman, George Brett, Gene "Doc" Broadman, and Jack Allen. The support team included John and Douglas Driggs, members of Gary's family.

Weather is the joker in the Tetons. Unfortunately, the weather was terrible for most of this trip. They tried their hardest but eventually pulled up stakes and returned home. They did learn that such an expedition was within their ability at a more advantageous time.

Summit of a Teton peak, Wyoming. Danny Kleinman, Gary Driggs, George Brett, Gene "Doc" Broadman, Douglas Driggs, Jack Allen, John Driggs (Kachina Archives)

Climb On

There were some fine climbers in my generation of Kachinas. The best two were probably Gary Driggs and Ralph Pateman (about whom I have already written). Not only did Gary acquire the skills but he also had an obsession for the sport beyond the rest of us. The climb I remember most clearly with Gary was to a mountain named SH in the Kofa Mountains located in western Arizona, not far from the state border with California.

Gary recruited Bob Radnich and me to join him on the climb. He also brought two friends as a support team. Gary must have given quite a sales pitch to me and Bob since neither of us was prepared for it; we had not climbed in a year and a half. Nevertheless, we hiked into the area and camped at the base of SH. Bob and I knew we were probably in over our heads when we saw an up-close view of the peak. It stood alone, a thousand feet above us with a sawtooth ridge at the top—scary. But we were there; we might as well try it.

Gary Driggs (Kachina Archives)

51

SH Peak in Kofa Mountains, 1951, off Highway 10 between Phoenix and Los Angeles (Kachina Archives)

SH in the Kofas

We began around five thirty the next morning and climbed all day, returning to the starting point by nine that night. Most of the climbing was of medium difficulty until we neared the summit. Gary led the whole way since Bob and I were rusty with our skills. One pitch was quite difficult. We knew from written accounts that a Sierra Club party had turned back at this point, but Gary managed to continue, with us trailing behind him.

When we were on the summit ridge, we knew we were right to see it as scary from below. I had never seen anything like it. It sloped up at a thirty-degree angle—which was okay, except that the narrow rocky ridge offered no anchor spots. Every rock was loose. This meant there was no way to tie down the safety rope. We were tied together, but if one of us fell, the other two would need to jump off the other side of the ridge. Then hanging hundreds of feet in the air, they had to find a way to climb back up, all the while keeping an equilibrium with the other climbers, lest one side would pull everyone off. I know it is difficult to picture. Suffice it to say, it was almost impossible; we just had to keep from falling.

I considered Bob Radnich the daredevil of our group. He would jump from the highest cliff when we went swimming in canyons or show his fearlessness in other ways. But this ridge was too much. Bob didn't want to go on toward the summit. Gary pleaded with him to reconsider, and I insanely conquered my own fear *just enough* to agree with Gary. We crept along the ridge to what seemed to be the highest point. But no, the true peak was across a chasm that would require us to rappel down 150 feet and then climb up another difficult 250 feet. It was clear that we could not cross the chasm and back before darkness fell. This time, the vote was two to one, and Gary had to agree to retreat with us.

The climb down was slow but not hard, and it was turning dark as we reached the last rappel. We had seen some of the pitons left in the mountain by the Sierra Club from several years ago. When we came upon one near the end, Gary was ready to trust it to hold us on the rappel. But Bob and I insisted on pounding a fresh piton into the rock and running the rope through both. Bob was last on that rappel, and halfway down, he suddenly dropped about eight feet. We knew one of the pitons must have just given way, and without the second piton holding, Bob probably would have been badly injured. We finished well after dark with just enough energy left to eat a little food but not enough to talk or even think about the climb, just scary dreams that night.

As well as Gary Driggs, the group of boys who followed mine included Charlie Scarborough, Gene and Laverne Prock, Danny Kleinman, George Brett, Jack Allen, Chuck Soul, and Doc Broadman. During the second year of their time, the Kachinas began to dissipate. I don't know how that happened; I was off to college. Others will have to tell that part of the story.

There have been two reunions of the Kachinas. The first was in Flagstaff at the home of Lee Pedrick. There was a good representation from the first generation, including Ben and Lee Pedrick, Dick Hart, Ed George, and Bill McMorris. Representing the second generation were John Goodson, Gary Driggs, and me. There was a day and night of great storytelling from our many exploits. Clearly, the early Kachinas had the most impressive climbing stories, and we had the infamous expeditions. The same was true at the second reunion in November of 2004 at Gary Driggs's house in Paradise Valley. This was a two-day event that included dinner, revisiting Pinnacle Peak and Echo Canyon on Camelback Mountain, and lots of storytelling.

At both gatherings, the keen importance of how the Kachina experience shaped each and every one of our lives was obvious. All of us seemed proud and happy with our chosen careers, and all of us could trace the impact of the Kachinas on our personal character development. I know about some of the careers that other Kachinas had pursued: lawyer, judge, minister, commercial artist, editor, director of a large search and rescue agency, banker, teacher, engineer, and coach. As I came to understand how important this teenage experience was for us, it began to shape my interest in working with young people in both my volunteer and career efforts.

Part Two

The Kachina Legacy

Transition to the Arizona Mountaineering Club

The first part of the Kachina legacy was carried forward by Doug Black, who was a Kachina when the group was winding down. In 1955, Doug helped start the Arizona Mountaineering Club (AMC). At first, the AMC offered an annual climbing school. Eventually, that developed into a biannual school, a rescue team, an advanced climbing school, and many other organized outings that took place all year round. They participated in expeditions to the Alaska Range, mountains in South America, and Mount Everest. The AMC carried the torch high for mountaineering in Arizona.

Newer Kachina logo (Kachina Archive)

Formation of the Pateman-Akin-Kachina (PAK) Foundation

The second legacy of the Kachinas began at a funeral in Phoenix. Ralph Pateman was killed in a helicopter crash while serving as an officer in the United States Marine Corps. Perhaps a dozen of the Kachinas attended his funeral. After the ceremony, his widow told us that he wished his ashes to be scattered from the Camel's Head. Would we honor him by completing his wish? Several of us agreed immediately to do so. We assessed our tools—yes, someone had an old climbing rope, and someone else had a couple of carabiners. That would suffice for an easy route up the mountain. So on that hot May afternoon, we rendezvoused at the Camelback parking lot—the Kachinas, Ralph's widow, and his best friend, a fellow marine.

Now it was time for a serious conversation. Who would make the climb, and who didn't feel in shape to do so? I think six or seven of us decided to go. After the first pitch, which was an easy climb, two dropped out. It was understandable; it was hot, and only one or two of us had climbed in many years. The remaining four of us struggled to the top without making fools of ourselves, except for a bizarre moment when Bob yelled, "Hey! Pass Ralph up here!" Ralph's ashes were in a metal container that was then thrown up a few feet. Thank god it was caught.

Finally, we reached the summit. Someone broke out a bottle of blackberry wine that had been Ralph's favorite drink when we were teens. We broke open the container, threw Ralph's ashes to the wind, and then toasted him as we passed around the bottle of wine. We made our way safely down, even though the rope we used was old and should not have been trusted for the rappel, but we had no choice.

When we reached the bottom, we were dehydrated and exhausted. However, Ralph's widow and her friend were waiting for us with a large pitcher and glasses. Ah, we would have paid a lot for a large drink of water. Oh no, we gagged on the liquid—martinis? Another time, we would have enjoyed it, but all we craved was ordinary water.

We journeyed to a nearby Mexican restaurant for water and some food and to talk. After toasting Ralph once more, John made a proposal to start a program that would let this generation of young people, including our own children, gain some of the experience we had—great idea but only a vague thought of how that could be accomplished. John volunteered to take on the formation of a nonprofit foundation to that purpose.

PAK Challenge

Challenge group on top of Mount Baldy in northern Arizona
(Dale Childs, PAAK Challenge Archives)

Now the question was, what would the program look like? We worked that out over a period of a year—about 1971. John, Bob, Stan, and I started meeting to brainstorm ideas. One key decision was not easy to resolve. Would it be for boys as was the Kachinas? Or would it be for boys and girls? John had yet to make the transition to the present era. "Girls," he said, "aren't capable of the rigors and mental strength that would be required." Since I had been working with both sexes in churches with outdoor programs and work projects, I knew girls were capable if they cared to join the effort. Eventually, that view won.

We weren't going to get very far if we didn't have enough equipment to outfit at least a dozen youth. I remembered Jack Abert; he lived across the street from my family when we lived on Monterey Way in Phoenix. Jack worked for AiResearch at the time. In his garage and backyard, he was always experimenting with building frames for backpacking. He was learning how to weld aluminum into a frame, a by-product of his work with airplane materials. I worked for him part time for a few weeks one year when I was in high school. In fact, Jack had encouraged me to take one of his aluminum frames on our Kachina expedition to Baja California. The frame wasn't suited to carry a good-sized load, and I fought the damn thing that whole trip while my companions laughed at my struggles. But at least I could give Jack feedback on his product when I got home. So now fifteen years later, I sought him out.

It appears Jack had the last laugh; he'd become the largest manufacturer of backpacks in the world under the label Camp Trails. He had sold a modified version of the small pack I used in Baja to the Boy Scouts as part of their line of official gear. He also crafted a much more substantial pack. Jack agreed to help us with our new program by donating fifteen large-pack frames and six two-man tents. After that, we received donations from the Akin and Pateman families, along with others, to purchase twenty good sleeping bags, camping and cooking gear, and first aid and climbing gear— most everything we'd need for a group of twenty people.

The next question was about the program: would it be for mountain climbing, or would it include a broader range of outdoor sports? We heard that Prescott College had a good reputation for providing a strong component of outdoor activities for their students. We tracked down the director of this department, Jim Stuckey, and went to talk to him about the program. Jim was articulate about the educational and personal growth advantages that resulted from a well-organized program. He invited us to send a group of youth for a four-day experience with Prescott College. The students we recruited were mainly from my church youth group, in addition to some others from our own families and friends. A dozen high schoolers, a couple of adults, and I all met Jim and four of his college leaders in Prescott. The first day was spent in the instruction of rock climbing in Prescott and climaxed with a seventy-five-foot rappel that ended next to a highway, guaranteeing a passing audience.

Rappelling off a granite cliff with Prescott College (Dale Childs, PAAK Challenge Archives)

The next day, we left Prescott. I was heading home for work, and the others were on their way to the Colorado River. They approached the lower part of the Grand Canyon on a rough road to Peach Springs. They brought with them small, twelve-foot rubber rafts, paddles, life jackets, food, cooking gear, etc. They launched the boats after a training talk and immediately faced two large rapids—sixes on a scale where ten is the most difficult rapid. I made this trip later, and I can testify that those rapids are a thrill. The group stopped to climb up a travertine canyon, and then they went back onto the boats for another few miles downriver and then finally camped for the night.

Rafting down muddy Colorado River in lower Grand Canyon with Prescott College (PAAK Challenge Archives)

The next day required more strength. The further they went down the river, the harder they rowed. It's usually easier downriver, but Lake Mead backs up to the lower part of the canyon, reversing the flow. They slept on the beach of Lake Mead that night and came home the next day.

The trip was a success on several levels. It was exciting for the students without being too dangerous. They learned a lot, from rock climbing to white-water rafting, group camping, and the geology of the Grand Canyon. They also learned about being a helpful part of a group when functioning in rough conditions requiring team work at every turn. And they saw college student leaders—young women and men who were competent and compassionate.

About two months later, our church youth went Christmas caroling at a rehabilitation center. About fifteen of them were packed into an elevator when it quit working, and they were stranded between floors. As the minutes passed, their claustrophobia escalated, and their cries for help went unheeded. Finally, firemen came to their rescue, pulling them out of the elevator ceiling to safety.

We debriefed their experience the next day. Duane Holloran, a psychologist and colleague in ministry, led the conversation. Some students remained cool, while others panicked to one degree or another. Duane asked the students who had been on the trip with Prescott College to raise their hands. Every person with their hand up had remained cool in that emergency. Up until that moment, none of us had even made that connection. It is true that experience in situations with risk can help prepare one for the next risky encounter so long as it doesn't cross over into total fear and panic.

There were a few more experimental outings that year, including backpacking trips to Mount Baldy in the White Mountains and other places. We began to include some of our own children on the outings—Mel Goodson and Mark Lefebvre. By then, we felt ready to begin our new program called PAK Challenge. Central High School seemed a logical school location for PAK Challenge to be hosted as a school club. It was in a neighborhood where we had contacts. John and I met with the school principal, Mr. Anderson, who was interested in the program but skeptical that students would respond to the idea. He accepted a bargain—we would advertise a meeting for interested students after school one day and test the waters. More than one hundred students crowded in for the meeting that day. We didn't bother to point out that about a third of them were part of my church youth group, and most of the rest were their friends. About one hundred of the students signed up on our interest list, which was far more than we could handle. There were also three or four teachers who were interested.

When we went back to the principal, he was convinced of student interest, but there were more hurdles to jump. There had to be a teacher to sponsor the club. Also, how could we choose only twenty students from the large number of kids who wanted to join? One teacher stepped forward. He did not want to be an adviser, but he would serve as the teacher representative until we found the right people. There were two other teachers who had attended that first meeting, Frank Plettenberg and Harold Baldwin, and it didn't take long for them to sign up. Frank was an art teacher, and Harold taught shop. Both loved the outdoors.

In a conversation among Frank, Harold, John, Dale Childs and me, we agreed on the composition of the first group. Many of the young people who had signed up were successful students, known to be leaders among their peers. We could have launched a rather elite group. Instead, we chose a cross section of students—some who excelled at academics, athletics, or social skills and some who were considered average, even struggling in school. This composition would be a fair test in measuring the impact of the program.

PAK Challenge was organized in the basic unit of a "pride[2]" with about twenty students and two to four adults. Two of the adults were teacher-advisers who were expert instructors for specific outdoor skills. The other adult "advisers" were there to help as needed. The idea was to have an adventure one weekend a month for the nine months of the school year. Each adventure would be unique, requiring a different set of skills such as backpacking, desert survival, rock climbing, caving, canyoneering, cross-country skiing, and white-water rafting. Summer expeditions were an option to go to places like Colorado, Utah, Hawaii, and Mexico.

---

[2]   As in a pride of lions.

Students preparing to climb into the San Juan Mountains in Colorado, 1974 (Dale Childs, PAAK Challenge Archives)

We divided the workload for our board. John would see to the legal requirements—forms required for the school, parents, and our board. I would assist Dale in organizing PAK Challenge. Other board members would help where needed.

We interviewed the students who applied and paired it down to forty students. So there were two initial prides. Their first weekend outing was with Dale Childs.

First Challenge Outing

Dale Childs was a member of our church college group. We had hired him part time to assist with the outdoor events that were part of our youth program. We offered Dale another part-time job with PAK Challenge as the coordinator. It was a huge job, much larger than we had envisioned. But Dale jumped right into the work. He was the glue that held everything together for the first two years. He was a model of reliability and had passionate care for the environment as well as for the welfare and personal growth of all the students. It would have been utter chaos without him.

Brent Roberts and Dale Childs (Dale Childs, PAAK Challenge Archives)

In Dale's words,

In January 1973, my work began. My duties included planning and leading monthly outings with twenty Pride 1 students from Central High School (CHS) as well as conducting weekly meetings with students and advisors to prepare them for each monthly outing.

Following an exhaustive student selection process during January of that year, our first Pride meeting was held atop Squaw Peak (now Piestewa Peak) on a sunny February afternoon in Phoenix. The students, two CHS faculty advisors, and three PAK Board members climbed the mountain together. At the summit, we introduced ourselves to each other and discussed the scope and goals of the new Challenge program. The positive informal meeting set the tone for the excitement to come in the months ahead. I recall leaving the mountain that day feeling positive about the future of the program and grateful for the opportunity to work with such an outstanding group of students and advisors.

On the heels of a Colorado River trip that was aborted due to severe weather storms in February, we changed our plans to what became our first successful outing: an early March backpacking trip to Seven Springs. That PAK outing, and others to follow, were planned with as much student input as possible. On several Wednesday afternoons prior to the Seven Springs hike, students met with me at Orangewood Presbyterian Church in North Phoenix. The church was the site of the "Loft," my attic office and storeroom for PAK's impressive collection of frame backpacks, sleeping bags, and other equipment. Since many Challenge students owned no hiking equipment, they first needed to choose and borrow a pack and sleeping bag from the Loft.

On the patio of the church, we reviewed maps of the area we planned to hike. We divided into small, cooking groups to plan meals and determine stove and fuel requirements for the outing. Each group designated a student who would accompany me to the grocery store to purchase food items and package them up prior to our departure. We discussed drinking water needs, footwear, clothing, and safety items to be brought on the outing. They also learned how to properly pack everything into the backpacks.

My responsibilities also included the completion of several administrative tasks for this and every outing. Communication with students and their parents was accomplished using a mimeograph machine, the postal service, and a telephone. In the days prior to the outing, I sent out schedules of our departure and return times to and from Orangewood, our base of operations. Since there were no PAK vans in those early days, we relied on parents, advisors and board members for transportation. I managed a budget for each outing, collected the monthly dues from students to cover the cost of food and gas, and established a safety plan to address possible outing delays and/or emergencies.

All this had been completed before the Saturday morning the students arrived at Orangewood to leave for the Seven Springs trailhead. I answered last-minute questions from students and parents, as a growing collection of colorful backpacks lined the sidewalk outside the church. Finally, everything was loaded into the vehicles, drivers were briefed on their destination, and our caravan departed for the trailhead—just over an hour's drive north of Phoenix. I remember thinking to myself, "At last, the Challenge program is under way!"

The spring weather was ideal that weekend. Thanks to the recent rains, distant hillsides were carpeted with bright yellow and orange California poppies. We hiked several miles along Cave Creek to our destination, a flat expanse of desert near the babbling stream where we camped for the night. Since several students had never camped in the desert, considerable time was spent learning how to set up the latrine, tents, and sleeping bags. Time was also spent teaching them how to safely use the cooking equipment.

The next morning, faculty advisor Frank Plettenberg led us to nearby Skull Mesa where we inspected the eight-hundred-year-old North American petroglyphs. Frank was extremely knowledgeable about the ruins, and gave us an impromptu lecture on the history of the area. Upon returning to camp we implemented the proper cleanup for a campsite—leaving no trace of our visit—then we hiked out to our vehicles and returned to Orangewood. Our first Challenge outing had been a success.

Dale Childs planning with students, 1973 (Kachina Archives)

This one-night backpacking outing was just the beginning of Challenge. In the months and years ahead, Challenge students participated in an exhilarating series of different wilderness experiences. There were whitewater rafting trips on the Colorado River, technical climbing adventures in the Superstition Mountains, cross-country skiing in Northern Arizona, long-distance

Cross-country skiing in northern Arizona, 1974, Cindy Lefebvre in the lead (Dale Childs, PAAK Challenge Archives)

bicycle tours, wilderness safety and first aid training, and much more. Pride 1 continued, and PAK expanded the program by organizing Pride 2 at Central High School in November of 1973, and then Pride 3 at the Downtown Phoenix YMCA in September 1974. During the years of 1973 and 1974, nearly eighty Challenge students participated in the three Prides. These were busy and exciting times as three separate outings were completed in each month of the school year. Unique programs were offered to Challenge and non-Challenge students during the summer months.

Now, some forty-three years after my first involvement with the Challenge program, I remain grateful to PAK for inviting me to work with these exceptional students and faculty advisors. I have lost contact with most of the students, and wonder how their Challenge experiences may have helped them as adults. The few I do communicate with lead exemplary lives. My two years in PAK affected me in positive ways that I can hardly express. All of us—adults and students alike—were learning so much about our inner strengths and abilities to both survive and thrive in this busy and challenging world.

Impact on Students

In Challenge, we expected the students to learn camping, hiking, climbing, caving, desert survival, first aid, etc. But there were other lessons the students learned—lessons we couldn't have predicted, at least not consciously. We watched students behave in ways that helped build trust and a sense of community within their groups—small acts of supporting one another, helping to bear one another's loads, that sort of thing. And they also let others know about the fear they felt when approaching an obstacle. Once the mission had been completed, they'd talk about overcoming that fear. They would show up at meetings on their bikes, explaining that their group had decided that one small contribution they could make for improving the environment was to use their cars less and their bikes more. They would reach out in the darkness of a cave to take someone else's hand. We discussed how these experiences could carry over in dealing with the fears that we all faced in school or at home.

One day five of our student leaders came to me for advice. In a few days, they would be expected to assist with our climbing school during a weekend of rock-climbing training. They told me they were afraid, either of being on the cliffs or of the expectation of being a leader when they felt inadequate. I thought about their fears and realized they were not alone. Probably half our young people completed our climbing school but still had fears strong enough to never try climbing again.

Mark Lefebvre topping out (Mark Dusza, PAAK Challenge Archives)

I used this group of five to experiment with changes we could make in our school. So we went to a nearby area with large granite boulders. We played on the rocks for three hours, taking turns climbing a simple route up a rock only eight feet off the ground and then trying it again but without using our fingers—only our feet and fists. Then we did it again with blindfolds on. We played follow-the-leader, hopping from the rock to the ground. We climbed another route hand over hand so that we had to invent ways to get up the rock. Afterward, we sat in a circle and talked about our fears, starting with me.

This experience led to us inventing our own agenda for the first day of school—a mix of traditional techniques along with the ones we had invented. The second day included a rappel on the cliffs of our regular school. The expert instructor came to us at the end of the second day. "What did you guys do? The students were much better on the cliffs. They had more confidence, less fear, better balance. They were terrific."

We began to hear from the students about the significant impact Challenge experiences were having on their lives. Dee's story covers a long period of her life and the impact of Challenge from a longer perspective.

Dee's Story

Shortly after Renee stepped off the lip of the pinnacle to begin her 100-foot-roped descent, the bulky weight of her framed backpack flipped her upside-down. I watched, horrified. This was not the climbing experience I'd hoped for.

The previous night we had fallen asleep on the mountain watching meteors streak across the sky. It seemed like a fitting end to our high school club's graduation, a technical rock climb up Weavers Needle, which is a prominent and impressive 600-foot-butte in the Superstition Mountains of Arizona.

Weaver's Needle in the Superstition Mountains, east of Phoenix (PAAK Challenge Archives)

As a lonely and insecure freshman in high school, I would spend my lunch hour calling my mom so it looked like I had something better to do than eat alone. I suffered through the year, lacking the friends I craved, and with little interest in school activities.

My sophomore year, I attended an informational meeting that explained the group, Challenge. Each month we experienced a different, outdoor challenge. Time spent backpacking, rock climbing, overnight bicycle rides and cross-country skiing was all meant to teach us about ourselves in the world. The monthly dues were twenty dollars, for which I had to beg my middle-class parents. Finally, a deal was struck. I would take over the family laundry duties in exchange for the club dues. Little did I now this group would change the trajectory of my life for the better.

I began to test my limits and experienced the amazing outdoors for the first time. However, when I attempted the rock climbing challenge, I seriously considered quitting. My parents agreed to allow me to skip my high school graduation ceremony and attempt the rock climbing challenge, but only if I participated in the prior climbing instruction at the Carefree Rock pile. As my parents have often said since, "Challenge created a monster."

Deke Joralman at Miners Needle, Superstition Mountains
(Dale Childs, PAAK Challenge Archives)

For the first time, I began to rely on my inner strength and define far-reaching limits I never knew I had. How empowering to reach a summit after being frightened by the view from the bottom, even more so for a young woman!

During this first year in Challenge, I was discovering who I was, what I was capable of, and what was important to me. At the end-of-the-year slide show, a picture of me from our first trip surfaced. "Who is that?" someone asked. The changes were so dramatic—weight loss, contacts in lieu of glasses, and self-confidence—no one guessed it was me. I had officially found my place in the world.

My memory now consists of mashed-together moments: being snowed in and assumed lost on a backpacking trip in Oak Creek, the thrill of a Tyrolean traverse, a magical sunrise while scaling Mt. Rainier, and getting carried out after injuring my knee while attempting a small downhill section on non-releasing cross-country skis. Throughout every experience, I continued to gain knowledge of outdoor activities and ultimately, myself.

The deep relationships formed with other students were extremely important, but just as influential were the adults who facilitated our trips. The opportunity to spend time with enthusiastic, experienced adults was powerful. When my dad died during my college years, I was incredibly grateful for the quality time he and I had spent together on Challenge outings. The trips so affected him that years later he equipped our family for a backpacking trip to the bottom of the Grand Canyon. Memories like this helped my family through our painful loss.

In my senior year, I became a student leader. Two adults, Fred and Frank Hill (brothers, who are still friends of mine) were hired to teach climbing. When Fred couldn't attend an instructional meeting, David Hodson was asked to assist Frank. Because of that encounter, a couple years later David and I started dating which began a tremendously close relationship lasting over thirty-seven years . . . and counting.

The adventures continued through adulthood as David and I rock climbed, hiked and skied multiple locales. Learning from my dad's early death not to put things off until tomorrow, we decided to trek into Nepal without Sherpas before starting a family. Later, we exposed our two daughters to hiking, camping and ultimately whitewater rafting. The outdoors, providing both emotional and physical strength, has always been an important part of our many endeavors.

Although our daughters have not pursued outdoor activities as we thought they might, I believe that the exposure helped make them the strong independent women they are today. Our eldest daughter graduated from the University of Arizona and moved directly to New York City alone to become a writer—something I consider much scarier than climbing a mountain! Our youngest daughter pursued her love of travel by teaching English in Abu Dhabi. The circle of adventure is complete, as David and I now travel the world with them.

David and I continue to enjoy the strength of our solid and loving partnership in life and testing our limits is never far away. Through a brief stint of skydiving, frequent whitewater rafting trips down the Colorado River (as well as other rivers), or driving our Harley Davidson motorcycles across the Southwest, we continue to confirm our zest for life. Who would have thought it all began from exposure to a high school group? I believe the impact of Challenge will continue with future generations.

New Challenge Adult Leadership

After providing excellent leadership for PAK Challenge, Dale resigned in 1975. He left exhausted—but he left behind a strong organization, a cadre of capable advisers, and experienced students. Challenge also now enjoyed a good reputation in Phoenix.[3]

During the following few months, our volunteer advisers stepped up. We were not able to efficiently handle our high number of students and logistical tasks. However, we benefited by taking on the additional responsibility, which resulted in our advisers learning.

Brian Early, Ellen Lawler, and Becky Nichols (PAAK Challenge Archives)

---

[3]   About this time, the PAK Foundation changed its name to PAAK Foundation to recognize and honor the contributions of Ben Akin to the foundation as well as to our entire state.

In the spring of 1979, three of the advisers—Brian Early, Ellen Lawler, and Becky Nichols—proposed to the board that they become codirectors. That could be possible if we were able to fund their small salaries by enrolling more students— forty-one to eighty of them—along with an increase in student fees. The board thought long and hard, and they agreed to work on a plan that would allow us to begin this new chapter for Challenge in the fall. Part of the plan was to talk to the parents about the increase in fees and to arrange professional training in both climbing and group dynamics with other outdoor-focused groups. Jim Stuckey of Prescott College guided us to Rick Medrick of Colorado. Rick was a well-known expert trainer of leaders in wilderness education groups.

Challenge leaders at Reevis at the time of leadership transition (PAAK Challenge Archives)

Our plan was for Brian, Ellen, Becky, and me to split up. Brian would take one of Rick's classes, Becky and Ellen would take a different one, and I'd take a third one. We then would come together to plan the new program. Our idea worked to perfection, except that Brian fell in love and followed his heart to Colorado. So the three of us devised a plan anyway. Becky and Ellen proved to be terrific leaders, and the program thrived for seven years under their leadership.

Student and Advisor Training

We thought the students would be in Challenge for one year, but by the end of the first year, it became evident to us that we had many students wanting to go on for another year. At the same time, we realized that we could use student leaders to help with the program, and they would benefit from leadership training. So we created a program to train students how to become leaders and called them Mountain Lions. They were required to have at least one year of Challenge experience, and then they would be chosen for the role by the advisers.

In practice, most of their training was "on the job," usually during our weekend pride outings. However, we also organized events for both students and advisers to obtain more leadership training. Most of these events were weekend long and covered many different outdoor skills and dynamics. We found them to be very helpful.

Next are two of my own stories; the first describes a training organized for a group of leaders that covered many skills, and the second is a typical outing where an emergency required the skills of two of the student leaders on that trip.

A West Clear Creek Training

Walking in West Clear Creek (PAAK Challenge Archives)

After we had been operating a few years, we began to have special leadership trainings for student leaders and adult advisers. These outings usually took place in October.

We arrived at the trailhead on top of the Mogollon Rim at about nine in an October evening in 1981 or 1982. At an elevation of seven thousand feet, it was cool and very dark—no lights from inhabitants at all. We assembled our packs, and the group gathered for instruction. I told the group that we were going on a short but very steep and dangerous hike. We would move slowly, helping one another, but with no talking unless it was necessary. We began walking, our headlamps lighting the way. The ground immediately began a downward slope and then a steep drop into the black hole that was the canyon. We hardly needed the extra weight of our backpacks to urge us downward. In fact, we kept having to grab hold of tree branches and rocks to keep from falling. Sometimes it was only the hand of a companion that kept us safe.

Eagle and poem (PAAK Challenge Archives)

I am the mountains,
I am the valleys
I am the cool clear air
And the sparkling water.
I am the wind
Whispering through trees
On crazy canyon walls.
I am the eagle that soars
Effortlessly on outstretched
wings.
I am life, freedom,
Courage, and grace.
I am nature. . .
Come join me.

James R. Vanko

It seemed like a very long and slow descent, although I knew it was only half a mile, no more than an hour and a half until we'd reach the stream at the bottom of the canyon. I told the group we had less than a mile to go to get to our campsite, but it would be a lot of rock hopping, stream crossing, and continuous alertness needed to get there safely. About an hour later, we reached our goal. We pitched our tarps and tents to make camp under the steep walls of the canyon. Sleep came quickly.

We woke up to a gorgeous sight. Through the leaves of the trees around us, we could see the red rock canyon walls rising hundreds of feet overhead. It was an enjoyable morning of eating breakfast, sharing our feelings about the crazy night hike, and absorbing the natural beauty around us.

Log crossing at West Clear Creek; Ellen Lawler leading a student (PAAK Challenge Archives)

Our day was filled with activity, all within a mile of our camp. We played some problem-solving games and practiced making shelters—some with large tarps, some with small tarps, and a third style using only the natural materials found on the canyon floor. We rigged a line above a large fallen tree that went across the canyon about ten feet above the stream.

We connected ourselves, one at a time, to the safety line and secured harnesses around our waist and hips. We proceeded to walk unassisted across the narrow tree that served as a bridge over the stream. Afterward, in a sitting circle, we shared our thoughts and experiences with leadership in the Challenge program. Then we pulled out topographic maps to see if we could locate our present position and identify other trails.

After a late lunch, we practiced first aid by staging a simulation crisis. One of our adult leaders told the group that Ben Avery, one of our highly skilled advisers, had been hurt while he and two other advisers were setting up a first aid scenario. "He hurt his leg, how badly we are not sure. It doesn't look good. Let's see how they are doing," the adviser told the group.

Ben Avery (PAAK Challenge Archives, possibly an *Arizona Republic* photo)

Well, the "accident" was simulated. Ben wasn't really hurt, but he did a good job at faking a broken leg. Most of our group headed to the accident scene, but there was one student leader who stayed behind for a few minutes to put away food. When he came up to the back of the circle of people surrounding Ben, he heard people saying Ben's leg was broken and that we would probably need to get help to evacuate him out of there. That student didn't wait to hear any more. He scurried up the trail to where we had parked the vans. He had the key to one of them. (He'd moved it as part of our preparation for the trip.) He jumped in and headed out on the dirt road and then to a paved road to the closest town, Strawberry. There, some people helped him call the local search and rescue group in nearby Payson.

Earlier, I had hiked out of the canyon as the group prepared lunch, for I had responsibilities in my church. So I was at home when I received a call from the young man who drove to town, telling me that Ben had broken his leg and that rescue groups were on the way. I knew that there was going to be a simulation, but now I believed the problem happened while they were setting the scene. The group must have sent word for a rescue. I didn't realize it was one boy who had jumped to a conclusion—big time.

Ben Avery was a close friend of Hattie and Bruce Babbitt, who was the governor of Arizona at this time. Still unaware that there was a misunderstanding, I thought it better for his wife to hear about Ben from me, rather than from the television, so I called them. I think the governor would have called in the National Guard if the Payson Search and Rescue had not been able to handle it.

Our main group was finishing off the simulation when they were surprised by the appearance of a rescue group. The rescuers were not exactly happy when they saw Ben was fine. It was an embarrassment for us, but it was another teaching opportunity. Every time we had an accident or a foul-up in communications, we debriefed the incident to the whole group back in Phoenix. Each time, we learned a lot. We knew we were doing a good job on safety since we had very few accidents, none of them life threatening. And we knew that our students were learning from the incidents. We referred to the incidents in later trainings, and we could tell it was helping, for our student leaders often incorporated the learning into their own teaching.

Jay Cone's Story

The ill-fated outing must have taken place near the end of the school year. I remember that I was going to have a final exam for one of my high school classes on the Monday following the weekend hike. The month of May is significant because there was a higher than normal spring runoff from the snowmelt that fed Cibecue Creek. As it turned out, the unforeseen conditions in the canyon caused by the high-water levels meant slow-going for our hiking group of high school students, a sleepless night for about a dozen parents in Phoenix, and a re-scheduled final for me.

Planning a trip (Dale Childs, PAAK Challenge Archives)

I was one of two student leaders who planned the hike. Those who knew the area had described the hike as an easy trek that followed Cibecue Creek downstream through a canyon. The trail started on Native American tribal property and then snaked back and forth across the creek, ending at a road where the creek empties into the Salt River. We calculated the distance on USGS topographic maps and it looked like an easy day-and-a-half trek.

Two adult chaperones joined us and drove us north from Phoenix in two cars after school on Friday. Frank Plettenburg was an art teacher at our high school and a sponsor for the Challenge club. Frank had accompanied the group on dozens of wilderness adventures. The other chaperone was Dr. Kramer, a father of one of the newer members in the Challenge club. Dr. Kramer loved the outdoors and this was the first hike for both him and his daughter with our group.

We paid a fee to the Fort Apache tribe who owned the land we would camp on that Friday night. When we reached the campsite, we emptied our gear and started preparing dinner while Frank and Dr. Kramer went to drop off a car at the point where we would exit the canyon on Sunday. The plan was to sleep at the trailhead Friday night, hike all day Saturday, and sleep in the canyon Saturday night. We would end the hike at the point where Cibecue Creek empties into the Salt River—where Frank parked his car. The drivers would then head back to the trailhead to pick up Dr. Kramer's car and return to collect the group. We planned to be back home early Sunday evening. Early enough—I had convinced my parents—to study for my final.

Walking in a side stream off the Colorado River (Dale Childs, PAAK Challenge Archives)

We started out early Saturday morning at a leisurely pace under clear skies. Because we were going to be in and out of the creek all day, we elected to hike with sneakers rather than slog along the trail in waterlogged hiking boots. The land is flat at the trailhead, but as you walk downstream toward the Salt River, you end up inside the canyon walls that had been formed by the creek. By Saturday afternoon we found ourselves walking in the creek much more often than we had anticipated. As the canyon walls became taller, opportunities to walk on land became scarcer. As the sun started disappearing behind the western canyon wall Saturday afternoon, we realized that we had not made as much progress as we had planned. A few of the group were having difficulties balancing on the slick rocks in the riverbed. Someone had twisted an ankle and we felt lucky to have Dr. Kramer with us.

Apart from the dramatic canyon walls, the clear, cool creek that would supply us with clean drinking water, and the desert terrain that was in full bloom, we were most looking forward to reaching Cibecue Falls. The falls were a mile or two from the end of our hike and would be an ideal place for Sunday lunch. We had been told there were pools—both at the top and at the base of the falls that we could swim in.

We found a flat, grassy patch along a bend in the creek where we could make camp Saturday night. We built a campfire and pitched our tents. We changed into warm, dry clothes, relaxed to the sounds of the flowing water, and edged closer to the campfire as the dry desert air quickly cooled in the twilight. We talked through our plan for the next day, agreeing to get an early start since the constant trekking through the creek was slowing our progress. We also thought we could save time if Frank and Dr. Kramer hiked ahead of the group after we hit Cibecue Falls, so they could drive up to the trailhead and get the other car while the rest of us lingered at the falls. It seemed like a sensible plan, if a little unfair to them. We all agreed that we'd wait to decide until we reached the falls and checked the time.

At dinner that night, we had another setback. Someone had left a camp stove too close to the fire. Camp stoves work by the pressure created when the fuel is heated. In those days, camp stoves were designed with a safety release valve in case the fuel overheated. The release valve prevented the stove from exploding. Frank was tending to something near the campfire and he bent over with his back to the fire. He hadn't noticed that the unattended stove had started to overheat. When the release valve opened, a concentrated flame shot from the stove and caught Frank on his calves, leaving him with serious and painful second-degree burns. Dr. Kramer recommended that Frank cool his legs in the creek, but other than trying to ease the pain and keep the sunlight off his burns the next day, there was little else that could be done.

All day Sunday, the canyon walls became taller and steeper; the creek seemed to snake back and forth more than it had on Saturday. We began to wonder if due to the twisting and turning of the creek, we had miscalculated the distance. Just as worries about being delayed started to distract us from enjoying the magnificent surroundings, we heard a tremendous rush of water coming from around a canyon bend ahead of us. We picked up our pace, and felt a wave of relief and gratitude when we came upon the falls. We now knew that we were no more than two miles from the Salt River and Frank's car.

We played in the water, sunned ourselves on the rocks, and ate lunch—confident that we had only a couple of hours (at most) left to reach the Salt River. As agreed, Frank and Dr. Kramer finished their lunches and started out ahead of the rest of us. We stayed at the falls for another half-hour and then, rested and in good spirits, we headed downstream. After hiking a short while, we came around a bend to find Frank and Dr. Kramer walking toward us. We could see that they were wet up to their chests.

They explained that up ahead, the creek flowed into a pool of water that stretched across the canyon. They had made several attempts to cross the pool with their packs, but it was simply too deep, and the walls were not safe to traverse. They could see where the trail emerged on the other side of the pool, but they couldn't see a way to reach it.

Walking in a canyon stream, (Dale Childs, PAAK Challenge Archives)

We concluded that it would be too risky to bring the group and all our gear across the pool of water. We also realized that turning around meant another night in the canyon with no way to contact our families. Jacob Furgatch, the other student leader, and I volunteered to swim across the pool and make our way to a phone to let everyone know that we were safe. We had seen a gas station on the highway a few miles from where Frank left his car. Since neither of us knew how to drive, we planned to leave our packs with the group, so we could pick up the pace. We figured we could make it to a phone in two or three hours on foot and be back to the group before nightfall. Because he had appointments on Monday that would need to be cancelled, Dr. Kramer wrote down the number of his office receptionist and his nurse. Jacob and I packed a few snacks and some survival gear into a stuff sack. Jacob held the sack over his head and we both dog-paddled our way across the pool. The rest of the group found some land where they could rest, dry out, and wait for us to return.

We walked briskly once we picked up the trail again. We were deep within the canyon now with no line of sight beyond the next bend in the creek. We walked for an hour, but it seemed as if we weren't any closer to the Salt River. We approached every bend with hope and went around the corner, only to see the familiar and maddening site of yet more canyon. We lost sunlight by late afternoon and the cooling canyon air against our wet clothes didn't help our mood. By 6:00 p.m. Jacob and I realized that we needed to make camp. It would soon be too dark to make our way, and we would need what was left of the daylight to find firewood and a dry spot to sleep.

We suffered through a long uncomfortable night. We rationed what little food we had and took turns stoking the fire and sleeping. We wrapped ourselves in the plastic tarp from the survival kit and spend much of evening speculating about what would be going through the minds of our parents and the group we had left behind.

As soon as it became light enough to see our way, we set out. It was now Monday morning. We presumed that our frantic parents would have been on the phone all night with the PAK Foundation, and it was likely that some foundation members were driving up from Phoenix to search for us. We continued following the flow of the creek, confused about our location, but certain that we were heading toward Frank's car and a dirt road leading to a phone. We were less sure about what had become of our hiking group. What would they think had happened to us? How long would they wait for our return before doubling back? If they were on the move, what would they have done with our gear?

Late Monday morning, we heard a thunderous movement of water ahead of us. We came around a bend and realized we had finally come to the waterfall that we had been trekking toward all along. It was massive. We later learned that record snowmelt had created an unprecedented rise in the level of the creek.

The high water not only covered much of the trail, it had created a second waterfall upstream from the one we had been told about. Our sense of relief was short-lived. We now knew where we were, but we couldn't see a way around the falls.

Determined to exit the canyon and get word to our families, we chose a path along one of the canyon walls that looked to have good hand and footholds. The wall was slick from the spray of water coming off the falls, so we took our time. One person inching down the wall and the other pointing out nubs and cracks to move towards.

Downstream from the waterfall, the canyon walls gradually lowered revealing more of the sky and giving us a real sense that we were nearing the confluence of the creek and the Salt River. By midday Monday, we reached Frank's car and saw that someone had left a note telling us to wait. Jacob and I reasoned that anyone returning to find us would have to drive on the dirt road from the highway, and they would see us walking out to the gas station. We still had calls to make.

We made it to the gas station without seeing any cars. The person working at the cash register told us that some people from Phoenix had been in earlier looking for a group of hikers. The gas station did not have a payphone, so we used the dimes and quarters we had collected from the group to buy candy bars. I don't remember if we ever made any calls to Phoenix because shortly after arriving, we were reunited with Gene and a few others at the gas station.

Challenge vehicle (PAAK Challenge Archives)

Jacob and I joined Gene and a group of volunteers he had assembled late Sunday night. We piled in the car and drove north to the trailhead. The group of us started down the creek trail again carrying ropes, first aid kits, and extra food. We periodically used our whistles and called out, hoping that Frank and Dr. Kramer had decided to double back and would hear that help was on the way. We heard the other group respond to our whistles and yells long before we could see them, and picked up our pace in anticipation. The reunion was emotional. Frank's leg had started to blister. He had fashioned a walking stick out of a tree branch and was limping noticeably. The group had divided the gear Jacob and I left behind, each of them carrying what they could. We rested for a bit while Jacob and I collected our packs, tent, sleeping bags, clothes, and trash from each of the other members of our group. I distinctly remember that no one spoke during the entire three-hour drive back to Phoenix.

As I write about the Cibecue Creek hike some forty years later, many of the feelings and images remain vivid. At the same time, there are regrettable gaps. I don't know if anyone kept a journal, and there are no photographs. I am no longer in touch with anyone else who hiked the canyon that May.

I have been thinking a lot about what we dealt with and how we responded as a group of teenagers. Jacob and I had been members of the Challenge club for most of our time in high school. We had been expertly guided on dozens of backpacking trips. We learned rock climbing skills, and orienteering skills. We had been trained in desert survival and the basics of search and rescue. Most importantly, our experiences with Challenge gave us confidence to lead, collaborate, and persevere. What I remember most clearly is that no one panicked or at any time felt like we were in over our heads. Each new obstacle was merely a problem that the Challenge club had equipped us to solve. In retrospect, the Cibecue Creek hike was the real final exam for me that year.

Part Three

Special PAK Programs

Summer Adventures

There were several summer adventure trips that were open to Challenge and other high school students, ranging from one to four weeks in length.

- Green River adventure, Green River, Utah: white-water rafting and hiking

- Two Wind River adventures, Wind River Range, Wyoming: mountain climbing and hiking

- Two Colorado adventures, the Colorado Rockies: hiking, climbing, and white-water rafting

- Island adventure, Hawaii: hiking, snorkeling, and sailing

- European adventure, Germany, Austria, England, Italy: hiking

Representatives of summer programs: leaders, Hawaii, girl taking a break, group of leaders, Bob Radnich at base camp, spelunking (caving), climbers in snow (Ben Pedrick, Wynn Akin, Dick Hart), Kate Leonard rappelling, cycling (from PAAK-Challenge Archives)

Special Service Projects

PAK was a key partner in two special service projects: the Grand Canyon Camelthorn Project and the Clifton Flood Project.

Grand Canyon Camelthorn Project

In the early summer of 1974, the scientist in charge of the Grand Canyon's inner canyon, Dr. Roy Johnson, faced a problem. An invasive weed threatened the beaches of the canyon—a foreign plant called "camelthorn," which could make it extremely difficult for humans to camp on the beaches. Camelthorn originated in the Middle East, where it was used to form brush fences to corral animals. At maturity, it stood about three feet tall with needlelike sharp thorns at the end of its branches. There's only one type of animal that can eat this pesky plant—camels, hence the name "camelthorn." Somehow this plant managed to travel thousands of miles to find a new home in northern Arizona, including the Grand Canyon.

Camelthorn bush (Dale Childs, PAAK Challenge Archives)

Roy's problem was that he could not use a chemical weed killer in a national park without an act of Congress. He decided the solution was to use volunteer workers who were willing to pull out the plant by hand. These volunteers needed to care deeply about the environment, have their own leadership, and be willing to follow directions. They would also need to pay for large rafts, expert river guides, and their own food and transportation to and from the Grand Canyon.

Fortunately, one of the members of the advisory board for the Grand Canyon Park was a longtime friend of Roy's and an expert outdoorsman. Ben Avery possessed some of the answers. Ben was also a member of the board of the PAK Foundation that sponsored an outdoor leadership program for high school students called PAK Challenge. And I was president of that board. It seemed to Ben and me that Challenge was the answer.

However, there was another obstacle to jump—how would we get students out of school for a week or two in October, the only time the project could happen? It took one more connection. I had volunteered with a gifted student program at Central High School in Phoenix called Seminar. Sylvia Orman, director of Seminar, was excited by the prospect and willing to work out the educational part to satisfy her superiors. Additionally, Jack Rickard, Jessie Hise, and Paul Hatch all signed on as teacher-advisers.

Then we worked out more of the logistics. The camelthorn removal piece would require ten days on the river. We could break the trip into two pieces with two groups of volunteers, one for each five-day section.

Roy took the plan to his board and superiors. To our delight, they not only approved the plan but two Grand Canyon rafting companies, Sanderson and Arizona River Tours, each donated the use of one of a giant raft plus one of their professional river guides as well to support our mission. That took care of a huge part of our equipment needs, and with it, we could envision a group of ten students and two teachers for each five-day period on the river as well as staff for the whole trip. Ben and my PAK board had no trouble approving the plan, and Ben and I could be part of the staff.

Group hiking into the Grand Canyon for the Camelthorn Project (Dale Childs, PAAK Challenge Archives)

Sylvia and I agreed that the twenty students had to be in the Seminar program to be eligible, with priority given to Seminar students who were already part of Challenge. Students had to work on a project in science, art, history, or English before, during, and after the trip. Sylvia would also deal with providing the information about the trip to the school, the selection of students, and their parent permission forms.

Roy would direct the uprooting of camelthorn. The river guides would control the rafts, the river gear, and the safety on the river. Dale Childs, director of PAK Challenge, would direct the second group's camp on the South Rim and their hike down into the canyon. I would manage the coordination of all the elements. Sylvia had a student, Kathy Angus, who served as her assistant while she recovered from an illness. Kathy would help Sylvia with preparations, and then she would serve as my assistant while we were on the river. Roy, Ben, and the river guides would educate us on the history, geology, biology, ecology, etc., of the Grand Canyon. I would lead the evening campfire information sessions.

Loading large raft on the Colorado River
(Jack Rickard, PAAK Challenge Archives)

The first group of students and teachers would arrive on a Saturday in October of 1974, sleep overnight at Lee's Ferry, and launch the next day. They would travel downriver for five days to arrive at noon on the river near Phantom Ranch.

Then they'd hike out to the South Rim, stay overnight at the campgrounds, and go home the next morning. The second group would leave Phoenix on Wednesday, sleep overnight at the South Rim campgrounds, and hike into the canyon the next morning. They would pass the first group on the trail and arrive at the river about noon.

The trip was magical—everything we dreamed it could be and more. We launched the rafts from Lee's Ferry on Sunday. The rafts were huge, thirty-six-foot-long pontoon boats large enough to each hold fifteen people and all their gear. They were propelled by small outboard engines. And we were off.

We were soon in Marble Canyon, a marvel of high red and brown cliffs. The rapids through Marble Canyon are medium-sized, good as an introduction to rapids but large enough for a thrill. Marble Canyon did not have camel-thorn-infected beaches, so we could relax and take in the natural beauty.

The first night at camp was spent getting to know one another and reviewing the rules. From here on, we would follow a routine like this: breaking down camp and packing, eating breakfast, running rapids, stopping at beaches to work on the camelthorn, eating lunch, listening to our experts talk about the canyon, students working on their projects, setting up camp, eating supper, and having campfire conversation. For the student learning projects, one student might be taking photographs, while another was painting a scene of the canyon; another might be taking samples of the vegetation, while others were writing in their journals.

Central High students dragging out the Camelthorn plant
(Dale Childs, PAAK Challenge Archives)

The work was hard and lasted about four hours each day, sometimes on one beach and sometimes on two or three smaller beaches. We tried different methods of disposing the tough plant. For two days, we put the limbs we'd pulled out through a gas-powered mulcher and then placed the mulch in large plastic bags. We left the bags high on the beach, to be retrieved by a park service raft that would come later. Sometimes we would haul the branches above the high-water mark without bagging them. On some beaches, we would try to harvest the entire plant—including its runners, which could extend up to twenty-five feet under the sand. This was very hard to manage. It was early October, so the canyon wasn't at its most extreme heat, but it was hot enough to tempt many of us to jump into the cold river.

Partway down the river, we came across a cliff dwelling, the home of the ancient ones. The ruins were high above the river but an easy climb, so we could examine the ruins up close.

The next stop was where the Little Colorado River enters the Colorado. It was time to play in the warmer turquoise water.

Running the rapids, Camelthorn Project (Jack Rickard, PAAK Challenge Archives)

Everyone anticipated the rapids would become larger as we floated down the river. As we lazily made our way down, we began to hear noise. We couldn't see very far up ahead, only as far as a straight line across the river. The noise continued to grow until it sounded like a freight train coming closer and closer. When the noise became almost too much to bear, we saw over and beyond that straight line—it was a steeply dropping rapid with huge waves and tumultuous swirls of water. We headed for the side of the river with the main current and straight for the canyon wall, turning away at an angle to the wall just enough to avoid crashing into it. Our screams turned to laughter as we emerged. It was a thrill every time we came to a large rapid.

Downriver to the next site (Dale Childs, PAAK Challenge Archives)

The current on the river through the Grand Canyon comes in long stretches where the flow is slow; it drags down the tempo of everything else. Folks settle down to bask in the warm rays of the sun. The only semi loud noise comes from the outboard engine. When the engine is switched off and people are quiet, you can hear clearly a variety of birds singing.

Of course, when the current is strong, it can be a challenge. Not only does the river get noisy through rapids but, between the rapids, a strong current also can push you toward rocks. Or if you don't keep the boat at the right angle, you may find the flow has pushed you into an eddy, and you must fight your way out of an upriver current to get back in the main flow. So just when you might have settled in for a slow-current nap, you become roused by river activity.

We experienced the force of the current one day when we were pulling up to shore to camp for the night. The first raft glided into the beach nicely, but the second raft wasn't angled quite right and had to be pushed on past the beach to head farther down the river. When that second raft managed to pull over, it was on the opposite side of the river. Half our people and half our gear had become separated by the river. Our people on the upriver raft thought they could solve the problem if one of them swam across the river with a line and pulled their raft across to join the other one. It was a good thing one of our guides was there to tell them the only safe solution: the upstream raft had to float down and across the river to join its mate. The current would have pushed the swimmer way down the river, and he or she would have been lucky to survive.

Sylvia, Jack, and I had been friends for a while. It was fun to watch them easily relate to their students, helping them with their projects and laughing at their stories. The two river guides (I forgot their names) were also great—professional in their skills with great leadership on the river as well as the camping. They were good storytellers with tons of information about the canyon. They obviously enjoyed the whole experience.

Digging out camelthorn (Dale Childs, PAAK Challenge Archives)

Typically, in the late afternoon, we established camp on a beach, unloaded the boats, and set up our individual sleeping sites. Most of us would rest or talk with others in our groups. A few would volunteer to help the guides prepare supper. After supper and cleanup, we'd talk about the day and plan for what was to come tomorrow. We would also bring up any concerns about how we were getting along. Finally, it was time for sleep.

Our schedule satisfied Roy. Plus, we were learning lots about the canyon from him, Ben, and the two river guides. The teachers thought the students were making progress on their projects. Everyone got along well and bonded with one another.

On Thursday, the last night in the canyon for our first group, we finished with a conversation about the hike out the next day. I said it was typical for the strong hikers to go ahead, even though it led to two problems. First, it was discouraging for the slower members. Second, if help was needed, the members who were most able to help would be gone up ahead. The group understood my suggestion and seemed to agree.

I found out later what happened from one of the advisers, Jack Rickard. As soon as the group began hiking up the steep canyon trail, the stronger hikers dashed ahead. Jack and a few others who hung back to help didn't see those early dashers again until well after dark, when the last of the line topped out on the rim. Meanwhile, those at the rear wound up carrying a lot of extra weight to relieve the weaker ones. Jack was in excellent shape, and I had never heard him speak about nearing his physical limits. I think this was the only instruction we gave that the kids blew off. There were a few of the students who had reached the top and waited for a while. Once they realized there were some people who needed help, they went back down the trail and helped those who needed a hand.

The second group reached the river soon after the first group had left. They were full of energy for the adventure. However, they were concerned they may have caused the death of a deer they had frightened. The deer had jumped off a cliff to avoid our group, and the students couldn't see the deer anywhere. Ben used this as a teaching moment. "The deer lives in this canyon. There's no chance he jumped off the trail without instinctively knowing exactly where he was going to land. If you had cornered him and he had nowhere to go, he would have turned on you and fought to get free, and some of you would have been hurt. This isn't Walt Disney's Bambi-land. This is nature where an animal's instinct is to survive. Remember that."

The Colorado River produces a great number of rapids from that point down the canyon. We were in our routine again: take on rapids, stop at beaches to pull camelthorn, take a short-side canyon hike, and listen to information from our experts as we floated on down.

The two largest rapids in the country are on this section of the river: Crystal and Lava Falls. They rate a "ten" on a scale from one to ten, with ten being the highest. Crystal is the first of the two, and we jumped out of the boats onto a trail that allowed us to view the whole rapid. It was scary. The river curves to the right, and the current goes through the boulders and down the center, straight into a hole—that's a spot in the river where water flows down from all sides into a hole. We piled back into the rafts and headed downstream, with the sound of the rapid pounding in our eardrums. We tried to avoid the huge hole but caught the edge of it, which tossed us around in our boats until we couldn't tell which way was downstream. We crashed through Crystal, with both rafts making it with all the gear and passengers—shaken up but still intact.

Heidi Angius on the Camelthorn Project (Dale Childs, PAAK Challenge Archives)

The pace of the trip for the first four days with our second group picked up speed. We negotiated small and large rapids, with Lava Falls tossing us around until we felt helpless again. We stopped at beaches to work on the camelthorn and stopped for lunch with the occasional side canyon hike, and students worked on their individual projects. By this point, the time among rapids, work on the beaches, and quiet floating downriver had diminished. The pace was faster, and the days seemed shorter.

What hadn't changed from the first trip was the evening schedule, beginning with unpacking the boats, then setting up camp, preparing supper, cleaning dishes, and finally time around the campfire to reflect on the day. The evening format drew the whole day together in a magical way. The days seemed like a perfect mix of hard work, exciting times through the rapids, and time for reflection while floating through the quiet sections of the river. Every evening of the trip ended with a sense of wonder and companionship around a campfire.

Another aspect of this trip made it unique. By October of each year, rafting in the Grand Canyon comes to a halt. The river flow drops because the downstream need for water diminishes in the fall and winter. There's insufficient flow for boats to negotiate the rapids. However, in the year 1974, an exception was made, apparently for our trip. The exception was ordered for a scientific purpose. There were no other rafts on the river, except for park service cleanup crews. Not only did we have special permission but I believe they also ordered the river flow to stay higher than usual for several days to allow us sufficient water for the trip.

We had the river to ourselves. I did not think about this during the trip. Only upon reflection did I realize it had added a special quality to our experience. Gone were the sounds of the voices from numerous groups of people along the route. Gone were the sights of campers on the beaches and many other rafts on the river. The canyon was ours for a few days, at least as far as human traffic was concerned.

Sometimes river trips end on a melancholy note with the return to more routine schedules of our normal lives. We had to leave this group of folks whom we'd come to know well. I did not experience that melancholy feeling at the end of this trip; I was ready to go home to my family. But I could hang out with many of those people after returning home. Also, I was looking forward to our stories being shared with families, friends, and schoolmates.

Central High students with advisers (Dale Childs, PAAK Challenge Archives)

The *Arizona Republic* published an informative article about the trip, and we gave a presentation in the library of Central High School one night. Students shared photos, paintings, and music. They also gave short reports on other projects they had completed and told stories of our adventures along with everything they had learned. It was a fun evening for the friends, parents, and teachers.

The students who chose to perform their own investigations concerning methods that might be effective in removing the dreaded camelthorn plant had come to the same conclusion as the scientific study led by Roy. They agreed that the only nontoxic chemical that could be applied to each plant to kill it was a saline solution. The large amount of salt water that had to be used was an unacceptable intrusion into the ecology of the canyon. Unfortunately, none of the methods we tried in removing the camelthorn made a difference. After a few weeks, it grew back.

Roy assured us that the project was a success because it demonstrated some of the methods that would not work. He said that he and his team of scientists would work in their lab and down on the beaches until they could solve the problem, at which time he would come back to us to volunteer for another attempt. That made us feel better.

We made a major mistake inviting news media to write about the project. It seemed that more than one congressman read about the trip and told the Park Service that they too wanted this same opportunity for students in their home district to be able to experience the trip. The Park Service threw up their collective hands. Rather than deal with an onslaught of such requests, they announced that there would be no more camelthorn projects.

Well, it was a terrific educational experience, and we had a grand time. That made the trip worthwhile. After all, how do you put a value on the sense of awe, wonder, mystery, or beauty, all of which we experienced in abundance?

Sundown on the river (Jack Rickard, PAAK Challenge Archives)

Clifton Flood Project

A strike occurred in 1983 at the large copper mine in Morenci, Arizona—it was a nasty drawn-out affair. It lasted three months, and then "scab" (a.k.a. strikebreaker) nonunion workers were brought in from nearby communities. Most of the striking workers lived in Clifton, a twin town close to Morenci. Even before the strike, the area was economically depressed. Now out-of-work folks were desperate.

Every day at 4:00 p.m., when a work shift ended, a line formed along a short road between the twin towns. Strikers, both men and women, stood on both sides of the road with their signs as they screamed at the passing vehicles carrying the strikebreakers. Some days, the strikers managed to stop the vehicles, and fights would occur.

One day a large fistfight broke out between the two groups. When violence broke out once more on the next day and the local public service officers could not contain it, Gov. Bruce Babbitt deployed National Guard troops. Even with this large group of enforcement officers, they could barely keep the lid on the angry crowd.

View of the Clifton flood from the air (courtesy of the *Arizona Daily Star*)

On Saturday, October 1, 1983, at 1:00 p.m., a flood came roaring down the San Francisco River and hit Clifton. Ordinarily, the river was a small quiet stream. But on this day, it grew to a monstrous eighty thousand cubic feet of water per second. And the next day, it grew to ninety thousand cubic feet. It hit the town so hard that one-third of the 126 businesses were destroyed and 47 of them were damaged. About 88 percent of the residences were destroyed or suffered major damage. No one was killed or badly injured because most people had been out of their homes at the time—shopping, visiting friends, or otherwise away from the crest of the flood that Saturday afternoon.

Governor Babbitt flew by helicopter to Clifton the next day to see the extent of the damage. He wanted to reassure people that help was on the way, and he got a close-up look at the devastation. After seeing most of it, he traveled to see north Clifton. This was an area upstream occupied entirely by strikers and their families. It suffered the most damage. No house was left untouched; three-fourths of them were devastated.

An angry crowd gathered around the governor. They let him know that they held him responsible for not doing enough to bring about a fair contract with the mine owners, which resulted in all the cops and soldiers gathered in the area. There were angry shouts like "*Now* you look at us! *Now* you come to help us when we are wiped out! We don't need you! Get the hell out of here!" or words to that effect. Officials and townspeople said later they feared the angry crowd would hurt or even kill the governor. Babbitt beat a hasty retreat.

As he flew back to Phoenix, he pondered what in the world he could do to help. One idea was that he could bring in some young people to help; the youth might defuse any threats the people felt from outsiders. Governor Babbitt called John Goodson. He knew that John and I led an outdoor program for high school students. He asked John if there might be any chance that our students could be organized and taken to Clifton to help folks dig out from the flood. John's answer was yes, and then he called me.

Since Becky and Ellen were such competent directors for the PAK Challenge, I called them for assistance. They agreed we could handle the governor's request even though we had only five days to prepare. We began to set things into action, formulating a plan and recruiting student and adult volunteers. This would require information flyers, registration forms, health forms, parent permission forms, transportation for up to fifty people, tools, camping gear (including tents), cooking gear, extra sleeping bags and pads, a nurse and first aid gear, radios, computers—the list seemed endless. Additionally, we'd need to establish a leadership structure with experienced people. And we would need money.

Watching the swollen San Francisco River in Clifton, Arizona
(courtesy of the *Arizona Daily Star*)

The response on all fronts was good. Media coverage showing the ravages created by the flood helped us. We had pools of students and advisers to pull from: PAK Challenge, two churches (Sunrise, where I was on staff, and Camelback Presbyterian, where my friend Jerry Roseberry was pastor), and the gifted students in the Seminar program at Central

High. These programs also provided us with contacts to the wider community for equipment and funding.

By Thursday night, we decided things were on schedule from our end, but we'd had no contact from Clifton. We decided that I would leave for Clifton early Friday with four experienced student leaders to scout conditions and set up for our work. Becky and Ellen would pull together the rest and lead a caravan of volunteers for a Friday night arrival.

When our scouting team arrived in Clifton about noon on Friday, we thought we had entered a war zone. We saw damaged homes as we drove closer into town. Farther down the road, in the business section of town, there were huge piles of mud and trash beside the road. We saw destroyed businesses of all sizes. Army-type trucks and heavy equipment were working their way through the destruction with helicopters flying overhead.

We located the police headquarters. It was packed with officers in different colored uniforms. We were shuttled to the desk of one of the men in charge. At first, he thanked us for coming and said they had all the help they could handle for now. When I told him that we were sent by the governor, his attitude changed. It went from "How quickly can I get these do-gooders out of our way?" to "Oh damn, what can I do with them? Better yet, who can I foist them off to?"

To our great benefit, he sent us off to talk to the superintendent of schools, Luis Montoya. He too was puzzled about what to do with us, but he was willing to talk. He learned quickly that we were only the scouts for a group that would total fifty by that night. I explained that we were organized and that we were self-sufficient in just about every way—we just needed direction about what type of work would best serve the community. I also made sure he understood that we would take direction from him and other emergency management leaders.

We looked over the school grounds with Luis, and he pointed out a campsite we could use, and then he suggested a route to drive so we could get the best layout of the town. Our tour of the destruction was both overwhelming and affirming— affirming because it was evident that these folks surely needed help. Many of the residents were either walking around their property in a daze or gathering in neighborhood groups on the streets to talk, all the while trying to dodge the National Guard trucks that were busy hauling mud and trash off somewhere. It seemed like there wasn't any organized *direct* assistance for the residents.

Losing a home to the San Francisco River (courtesy of the *Arizona Daily Star*)

The caravan of vehicles carrying the rest of our crew arrived about 7:30 p.m. We set up tents and a kitchen and prepared food for our hungry crew. Becky, Ellen, and I met with students and advisers—ones with the kind of experience that would serve us well. Then we gathered the whole group. The scouts and I attempted to explain the extent of the damage, which was now under darkness, but our descriptions seemed inadequate. I ended with "You'll see for yourselves in the morning. We don't need to say anything more about that."

Our mission was to help these people both physically and emotionally as best as we could. These were the guidelines we outlined for our volunteers:

1. We are here as guests. This is their town and their homes. Many of them are in a state of grief. They probably have lost their jobs, many of them have lost their homes, and many of them have no idea where they will go from here. They will accept our help if they see us giving off a positive attitude, which we can express by the way we smile and act. Above all, we must show them respect.

2. They will tell us what help they need. We will work hard shoveling mud, hauling off trash, or anything else they might want that's within our skill to accomplish safely.

3. We will be divided into work crews, each with a student leader and at least one adult adviser. Ask them if you have any questions. If they can't

answer, they'll try to find someone who can. Stay in your group; don't wander off. Everyone will have a buddy. Take care of each other. Crews will rotate turns for the cooking and cleanup after meals.

4. If you are hurt or sick or think you might be coming down with an illness, see our nurse.

5. We were called to be here by Governor Babbitt because he thinks we can help these people—help they wouldn't accept from other outsiders, help they are more likely to accept because you are young (most of you anyway). That makes it easier for them to believe you aren't here to take advantage of them or pity them, just to help them. We are privileged to be here.

When that was over and done with, everyone went to bed in the tents.

We were accepted by the townspeople tentatively at first, but it didn't take long to establish some trust. And we worked hard with the skills we had. We couldn't fix appliances—we weren't carpenters or plumbers. But we could use a shovel, a rake, and a wheelbarrow. Plus, we could use our hands. By noon on Saturday, we ran out of the type of work we could do for the nearby neighborhoods. And then things shifted.

Clifton flood destruction (courtesy of the *Arizona Daily Star*)

Luis asked the high school student body president, a sharp young man, to help us. He agreed to do so with enthusiasm. We had been told to stay out of north Clifton because of the anger of the strikers who lived there, but it was the most severely damaged area of the city. It was the area where the confrontation with the governor had occurred. There was very little money left in the union strike fund to support them. They were exhausted from fighting the flood and all the damage it caused.

The student body president refused to take no for an answer when it came to helping them. He said that, since it was the area that needed our help the most, the people there would welcome us with open arms. We took his advice, and our entire group headed for north Clifton—truthfully, we were more than a little scared.

We drove down the dirt road past buildings in shambles. Three men sitting on a porch yelled at us to stop. They came over to our line of four pickup trucks packed with students. "Who are you?" one of them asked.

When I explained who we were and that we were there to help them dig out of the mud or whatever else they wanted us to do, he said, "Well, I'll be damned. Welcome to Clifton. You're the only people who have even offered to help. And you came all the way from Phoenix? All right, we'll show you how to help." And they did.

I know from my previous work with flood damage that almost all the homes would be written off as a total loss by the government, and it would take a long time before they would help these people with new homes. So what would happen between now and replacement homes? These folks would live either with relatives or friends. Many of them would give up waiting and move to another town looking for work. They were in for a discouraging long time. The most we could give them was the support of showing that someone cared and that we weren't going to wait around for government officials to process all the red tape. We could help them salvage some furniture, pictures, and other items that had value to them, and we could do it now. Perhaps, depending on the situation, we might be able to clear out a room that was still structurally strong; that way, someone could live there for a while.

We helped them paw through the trash, carry stuff outside, dig out the mud, and sweep the floors. We worked side by side with these poor folks. Better yet, they were bossing us around and appreciating our letting them make decisions about the work. We packed up the trucks and our shovels—all of which were covered with mud—and started back to the main part of town, waving goodbye to the folks of north Clifton.

It happened to be about 4:00 p.m. when we drove back up the dirt road that intersected on a thirty-degree angle with the highway. We came to a stop at the highway, close to the notorious stretch of road where strikers had lined up behind a line of cops and the National Guard. The strikers were yelling curses at the strikebreakers when a procession of cars came down the highway. From our vantage point, we had a good view of the scene. Then a few of the strikers noticed that we had to come to a stop behind them. Word spread, and soon everything else came to a stop on the highway. The cops, the National Guard, the strikers, and the strikebreakers all looked over at us. Word must have spread about who we were because a round of applause started. First, a few people and then just about everyone was applauding and yelling words of appreciation at us. Miraculously, the willingness of the young people who came to help anyone who needed their help broke through the hatred and violence that the long strike and disastrous sudden flood had generated in the town. It was a moment for all of us to remember. And there was more to come.

Luis had arranged for us to shower in the school gym, followed by food. Dinner was followed by a debriefing, with everyone talking about their day. Then we gathered for closing conversation—lifting some stories from the day and sharing deeply felt emotions. I was glad the kids and advisers felt like heroes that day; they deserved it. Still, I felt it was my job to remind them that there were a lot of people in Clifton going through hell with this, and many of them were the true heroes.

We also saluted the Clifton student who knew his community better than many of his elders. He was the one who led us into north Clifton, where the need was the greatest. Despite the warnings from town leaders, the outcome was as the student predicted: we were safe and appreciated there.

On Sunday, we went back to work, scattering all over town to help where we were needed. We packed up camp, showered once again, enjoyed lunch, and stopped by the school to say goodbye to Luis. We traveled home, tired but with high spirits and lots of stories to tell.

The next day, Becky, Ellen, and I cleaned the gear and stacked it in piles. Some of it belonged to us, but much of it was borrowed, and we had promised to return it on Tuesday.

That night, still Monday, I received a call from the mayor of Clifton. "Gene," he said, "we had a town meeting tonight, and the room was packed. People here really appreciated the work your kids did. It lifted our spirits. The town council and all the people at the meeting voted to invite you all to come back this weekend. We still need help, and you guys are really good at it."

I think there was a long pause as I tried to absorb this call. I said I would consult with our leaders and let them know our answer the next morning. After telling Sue, I went over to Becky and Ellen's home to tell them. They got past the shock quickly, and we weighed the pros and cons, mostly trying to answer the question whether it was even possible to accomplish. We had to decide quickly, for we had only four days to prepare. I don't remember any more about the discussion, but we went back to Clifton.

Students hiking into Clifton to help flood victims (PAAK
Challenge Archives)

Local volunteers help Clifton folks to safety (courtesy of the
Arizona Daily Star)

We stuck with our basic organization plan, and we added a few new wrinkles. After checking with Luis in Clifton, five Bobcats were donated for us to use over the weekend. Bobcats are small front loaders, like miniature bulldozers, that can maneuver in small places—like front and backyards. They can move loads of dirt and trash more efficiently than we ever could have by hand. The father of one of our student leaders let us borrow his large flatbed truck to carry the Bobcats to and from Clifton. The folks in Clifton sent two professionals to Phoenix to drive the truck and trailer. From donated funds, we chartered a bus for the weekend. The Friday night caravan to Clifton now contained a busload of volunteers, three pickup trucks driven by adult adviser, and the truck and trailer. Once again, we totaled fifty youth and adults in our group.

This time, Luis had arranged for us to stay in the high school gym, which made "camping" less complicated than usual. We were received with open arms by the townspeople, and this time, we had a celebration before we left for home—a nice lunch and a parachute game that involved the strikers, law enforcement, and us. It was lots of fun.

We went home on Sunday afternoon feeling great and with more stories to tell. Three weeks later, we received a copy of a proclamation by the Clifton City Council declaring that a day in October each year would be designated as a day to remember not only the flood but also the volunteers from Phoenix who had come to their aid.

I reported to Governor Babbitt on the outcome of the project and suggested to him that a commission be formed to help the people of Clifton recover from the flood and strike. He formed such a commission with Secretary of State Rose

Mofford and other people who represented state and federal agencies, schools, businesses, and humanitarian agencies. I was also named to the commission. Two outcomes of this commission's work was that the US Army Corps of Engineers would oversee the building of a section of homes in Clifton for those displaced because of the disaster. Also, the Corps built a flood control structure to help with the next flood.

Summary of PAAK Challenge

The program PAAK Challenge slowed down and finally ended in 1988. About eight hundred students experienced Challenge over the fifteen years of its existence. We continue to hear stories describing the significance that Challenge has had on everyone's personal growth. Challenge was meant to be the heart of the PAAK Foundation. We wanted to provide a program that had an impact on the high school students—like we remembered from our time as Kachinas. Times were different, and students did not enjoy the freedom we felt at their age. On the other hand, Challenge provided more varied opportunities to experience the wilderness and a nice balance of adult advisers encouraging youth leadership.

The Kachinas were a testimony to the fact that, with expert training, teenage boys could accomplish astounding feats. PAAK Challenge was an affirmation that girls could match the boys in both the skills they learned and the courage with which they faced obstacles. Judging by our witness of the students' performance and the feedback we received from their advisers and parents and considering the students' reflection on the value of the program, we feel we accomplished our mission.

Part Four

The Challenge—Reevis Mountain School Connection

Siglinde Goodson

Backpacking in Guatemala

Can we ever revisit the past? It seemed so when John Goodson met Peter "Bigfoot" Busnack, who became his comrade and collaborator during the Challenge years and beyond. Their relationship was reminiscent of the lifelong friendships that the Kachinas had forged from their expeditions and mountaineering adventures.

John met Peter through one of the benefactors of the Challenge program. John Epert was the owner of a wholesale company of health food items who had generously donated provisions for several expeditions. When asked about advice on nutritious backpacking food, he recommended encouraging Bigfoot to talk to the students since he had a reputation for an unwavering commitment to healthy eating choices. In his lecture, Peter not only gave the students general nutritional advice but he also shared specific stories about how he had personally learned to forage for food in the wilderness by trial and error.

Occasionally, lessons had to be learned the hard way. Such an incident occurred when Peter was hiking around Lake Atitlan in Guatemala. He noticed some little red fruits lying on the ground, and they tasted quite delicious—a bit like cherries.

He must have thought, *Well, why pick up fruits off the ground when you can climb up the tree?* He comfortably positioned himself on one of the higher branches and feasted on the unexpected treat, eating the fruits—seeds and all. Leisurely watching the birds, he noticed that they also enjoyed the abundance of fruit, except they spit out the seeds. He hastily climbed down from his perch. At about this time, he broke out into a cold sweat and felt too dizzy to stand. He was barely able to crawl one hundred feet to the lake's lifesaving water. Peter's rationale for his inattention to detail was that he was only twenty-five years of age at the time.

Another experience gave Peter the opportunity to demonstrate the wisdom of always maintaining a calm and collected demeanor—even under the most frightening of unexpected circumstances. While backpacking in Guatemala, Peter hiked up to a mountain ridge. Upon arriving, an amazing experience awaited him. He had a front-row seat to watch the Pacaya Volcano erupt, shooting fountains of fire thousands of feet into the dark sky. While peacefully enjoying the splendor of the night, a stray dog that had followed him from the village started to whine, shiver, and tremble. Peter saw the cause of the animal's discomfort—a jaguar had joined them and was perched on a tree, also watching the fireworks.

It was time for a slow and cautious retreat. Peter remembered how quiet the tropical jungle was, with clouds moving through it like fog, causing images to appear and then disappearing. From the dog's behavior, Peter realized that the jaguar had been following them for quite some time, even though he never saw it in the eerie dense mist.

It soon became obvious to everyone that Peter had the makings of a commando. He was readily accepted into the Challenge program as an adviser, which allowed him to share with the students his experiences from living so many years as a wilderness entrepreneur.

From New River to Four Peaks

Peter started to consider the possibility of a solo trek across the Sonoran Desert, living entirely off the land. He asked John Goodson for counsel on map and compass navigation while traveling across the uninhabited terrain. It would have been reasonable for John to point out that, in the summertime, the desert is a burning inferno. It barely provides sustenance for its animals, water holes are few and far between, and no Boy Scout troop could come to the rescue if there were an emergency. John, however, had the heart and mind of a Kachina. "Right on, my friend. Fortune favors the bold."

John considered it a privilege and great fun to assist Peter in planning the impossible. It was most important to ascertain that the lone hiker could find his way across the vast silent land by relying only on his ability to translate map symbols into land features. Water hole locations need to be identified in advance. In the simmering summer heat, a hiker's life depends upon finding them.

Peter would begin his trek in New River on I-17 and complete it at the summit of Four Peaks. John offered to drive him to the starting point and bear witness to the hour, the day, and the fact that all Peter carried was a Pentax film camera, a tripod, and a machete—no food or water. The date was July 11, 1975.

Peter at the start of his solo trek to Four Peaks (Peter Busnack)

This must have been the beginning of what seemed like a truly foolhearted undertaking, and on some level, it was. However, Peter was prepared for this challenge. For years, he had hiked and foraged through the wilderness in many parts of the world. He knew the medicinal properties of desert herbs and which plants would be edible. He was comfortable sleeping under an open sky and had no fear of mountain lions, rattlesnakes, Gila monsters, or scorpions. His soul was in alignment with the land. His trek had the makings of a quest in which the hero proves his worthiness against terrifying obstacles.

On the first day, Peter hiked eight miles to his source of water. He found a wet spot in a dry wash—with a decomposing cow in it. About five inches of black muck was settled on the bedrock, with only about one inch of water on top of it. His options were few. It was drink or die.

Peter would later give the following description of this epic challenge:

It was late in the afternoon and I had been hiking since five o'clock in the morning. At this point, I was seriously dehydrated. Looking around, I found a large, thin, flat rock that I used like a shovel to scoop out much of that abominable muck down to the bedrock. Then I carried some large rocks to the area to create a circular enclosure—like a well—where water could collect without animals lying or dying in it. At this point, I was deeply exhausted and in a condition beyond thirsty, having felt no moisture in my mouth for some time.

I sat down to rest, expecting to hike two more miles to Fig Spring, the location of my next water hole. After about thirty minutes, I stood up with the intent to put my backpack on, however, when I woke up, I was lying in the dirt. I never felt my body hit the ground and this had happened twice. I realized that I was dying of thirst. I sat back down in a little bit of shade provided by a small mesquite tree and let my mind drift into a state of deep meditation. This was a very blissful experience. I asked for God's assistance. The miracle that saved my life arrived as a change of attitude concerning this evil-smelling sludge, plus a plan on how to make it drinkable by adding lots of horehound, one of the blessed herbs of the desert, and then boiling it. I now had liquid to drink, yet still could not make my own saliva. It took about two gallons of this horrible concoction until finally, at about 2:00 a.m., my body had sufficiently regenerated itself and I could feel saliva coming back into my mouth. The amazing and truly beautiful thing about these somewhat troubling circumstances was that at no time did I experience fear. I felt completely confident throughout this event, as well as all the days and incidents yet to come.

Peter walking through a cholla forest (Peter Busnack)

Even at night, the desert never cooled below ninety-five degrees, nor did the black muck magically turn into sparkling spring water. Yet Peter was at peace, ready to meet his next task. As previously planned, on the second day, he hiked two miles to an abandoned, one-hundred-year-old homestead called Fig Spring. Here, he found that squirrels, pack rats, and rabbits had been so desperate for water that they jumped into the well. They were unable to get out, which left their drowned bodies to decay in it. Peter stayed there all day to rest and boil a supply of the water that would sustain him throughout the next day. When Peter's memory visits that day at Fig Spring, he is amazed that he drank the nauseating liquid. Not surprisingly, this was the well from which he contracted hepatitis. Miracles occasionally come at a cost.

Fortune Favors the Bold (Peter Busnack)

According to Peter's testimony, the third day was extremely exhausting. He had to cover fourteen miles of difficult terrain, which included many canyons, to get to the next water hole. The combination of hepatitis and extreme heat made him feel sick. When Peter measured the outside temperature, his instrument registered 117 degrees in the shade and 135 degrees in the sun. The tool he used was a thermometer for developing photography—both accurate and durable—but it could only register up to 135 degrees.

Compared with the comfort and speed of covering the distance in a car, navigating just a few miles by map and compass is arduous and slow—especially over a terrain with no trails or friendly trail markers. In the desert, the hiker's place of destination seems to continually disappear into endless space while unrelenting heat challenges the strength of the body and mind.

In ancient stories, many times, unexpected relief is provided to a brave human engaged in a great challenge. That day arrived when Peter reached a water hole with bugs floating in it but no dead animals. What a precious gift for his survival! Relaxing from the day's hike while waiting for night to fall, he truly enjoyed this unexpected, thirst-quenching treat. Life was good. He knew that desert herbs would cure him of hepatitis. He continued on his journey, and three days later, he reached Seven Springs.

A reluctant farewell (Peter Busnack)

This is how Peter describes it in his own words:

I proceeded from one adventure to the next for about ten more days. I had one more close call with dehydration. As the trek progressed, I became more in-tune and comfortable with the environment. By the time I reached Four Peaks, I was ready to keep on going. Then I met a couple camping at Pigeon Spring. They offered to give me a ride, but I still wanted to climb Four Peaks.

What helped me to get up the mountain was that I ate some of the sweet honey I had extracted from a wild beehive set in the hallow of a sycamore tree. Before reaching the summit, lightning almost struck me. At that point, I recollected that I had a house payment to make, so I was finally ready to catch that ride back to Phoenix.

Peter immediately visited John to share his adventures with him. It was time to celebrate another great deed worthy of a commando in the Kachina lineage.

Zen and the Art of Land Navigation

John acquired his expertise with map and compass as a young reconnaissance officer while stationed in West Germany with an armored cavalry regiment. In this military setting, the success or failure of a mission can hinge on a leader's ability to read and use a map.

John Azmith and Peter Bigfoot planning the route across the rugged desert terrain. (Siglinde Goodson)

Years later as a civilian, John found himself in similar circumstances with his wilderness recruits from the Challenge program. Finding a safe route out of a canyon to a life-giving source of water can depend on the hiker's navigational skill. On Challenge outings, John occasionally referred to this topic. However, riding rapids and climbing mountains did not provide a suitable environment for teaching map and compass methodology. He decided it was necessary to formulate a new Challenge program that would give him the opportunity to train his young friends in a skill that was vital to their safety in an unknown wilderness terrain. He called it Zen and the Art of Land Navigation.

John Azmith teaching land navigation in his wilderness classroom (Siglinde Goodson)

John invited desert survivalist Peter "Bigfoot" Busnack to be his companion and second in command. Everyone called him Bigfoot because they were amazed that he handcrafted his own shoes since his size was commercially unavailable. By a similar process and as a sign of respect, John received the honorary title Azimuth because he was always talking about *shooting the azimuth* when it came to setting the direction of travel on a compass. An off-topic item worth mentioning is that John always preferred the spelling *Azmith* when referring to himself.

At these times of their lives, Peter was a new-age revolutionary, and John was a practicing legal warrior. Their friendship was a harmony of opposites based on profound mutual respect. Obviously, the table was set for both students and teachers to have great fun.

The new program was initiated on Columbus Day 1976. They chose this day to celebrate the life of the world's worst navigator. The program closed ten years later when John decided to retire from active wilderness duty. During this period, no two weekends were ever the same; but eventually, a basic format emerged.

John scheduled his workshops twice a year over a three-day holiday. At the beginning, only high school students participated; but gradually, adults who wanted to improve their navigational skills also joined. Combining the two age groups worked out to everyone's advantage. In this environment of "experiential education," no test scores or diplomas were necessary. The process of learning itself was fun and exciting and was greatly enhanced by John's ability to dramatize his presentation with narratives and colorful stories.

On the designated weekend, all participants usually caravanned from Phoenix to Globe. Cars were left for safekeeping at Jim Tidwell's Spring Creek Store on Highway 188, milepost 233. From there, it was only a short, half-mile hike up to Campaign Creek Draw for the night's camp.

The first day's instruction took place with the students seated on a flat area around a windmill. On the agenda were the fundamentals of map reading and compass application. John enthusiastically expounded the merits of checkpoints, contour lines, and azimuths with due consideration of magnetic north, highlighting the following six basic principles of land navigation:

1. Be certain of where you are.

2. Know with the preciseness of a saguaro needlepoint about your destination.

3. Plan your route carefully in advance.

4. Select checkpoints along the way to verify your progress and that you are on the right course.

5. Have objective evidence from your relationship to nearby mountaintops and sturdy landmarks that you are where you think you are.

6. Always be aware of your correct azimuth at all times.

The second day's assignment was for the students to plan a route up Nonesuch Mountain. Interpreting contour lines, checkpoints, and precise azimuths is easy in a classroom; but when traversing across the open land—as well as going up, down, over, and through the wilderness—the same tasks become challenging.

The lower Sonoran Desert has no dramatic features of vegetation or terrain. Scrubby mesquite trees, catclaw bushes, and occasional saguaros provided artistic ambiance but did not give navigational support. Since the landscape offered few visual clues, it was challenging for the students to stay on course; they hiked many miles across the rugged desert terrain, having to rely on their skills with map and compass. But what a thrill it was when they finally walked up to the water hole or to the campsite, which many hours ago had only been a small symbol on a map.

Compass (Gene Lefebvre, PAAK Challenge Collection)

Even Peter felt the strain of this navigational assignment. He candidly admitted that climbing uphill with a pack on your back while navigating with your compass, keeping track of your map, and identifying map features along with the hot sun truly made for a long day. John finally agreed that carrying all their gear for the weekend while trying to decipher map and compass directives was not practical, and he arranged for everyone's backpacks to be transported from campground to campground. This development was surprising since easy comfort was never considered a significant aspect of the program. It just was not commando-style training.

One year, the month of March brought a cold drizzle to the spring workshop. Most of the assembled participants were caught off guard and carried no rain gear in their backpack. Half of them quit and departed immediately. Even Peter dared to suggest that retreat was honorable. John was unperturbed and carried on with the remaining diehards. Peter had no choice but to spend the next three days shivering in a modified garbage bag "raincoat." Over this long weekend, everybody learned that if you go on an adventure with John Azmith, there will always be an element of dare somewhere.

Both teachers approached their respective fields of expertise broadly. For example, researching the properties of cacti had initially not been on the curriculum, but it certainly would enhance the students' ability to sustain themselves in case they ever got lost. So it was added.

To cite Peter's own testimony,

> I was in the early stages of experimentation. During some outings, we learned that adding red thorn prickly pear cactus in the evening's camp stew made some of us sick; I eventually found out that the white thorn variety is a powerhouse of energy. When cooked in water it produces a slimy drink that will give a hiker stamina for a whole day's activity.

Obviously, the usefulness of cacti as a food is limited.

Since early adulthood, Peter had always been eager to learn how to maintain health naturally without pharmaceutical products. This led him to the study of Jin Shin Jyutsu, a Japanese form of fingertip acupuncture, while he researched the medicinal properties of Sonoran Desert plants. On outings, he was well prepared to treat medical emergencies; blisters from new hiking boots were the most common. In those cases, the hedgehog cactus produced miraculous results, even on the most painful wounds, as well as in soothing sunburn.

Evenings around the campsite were always memorable and quite entertaining. Each teacher made a specific contribution to everyone's enjoyment. The effects of "bow and drill" friction have a rational, scientific explanation. Yet to watch Peter patiently kindle forth the first sparks of a live flame from tufts of dry vegetation felt like sorcery—like the ritual of ancient magic—especially when the coyotes participated by howling in the dark.

When all the camp activities gradually quieted down, it was John's time to show off his skill as a storyteller. Many a student remembered drifting to sleep while listening to John's voice telling the heartbreaking tale of a black rabbit. It was John's rendition of a popular novel about a brave rabbit that took on himself untold hardships and sacrifices for the sake of the common good, only to learn near the end of his life that his great deeds were forgotten, and he had become politically obsolete. He was not looked on with gratitude and admiration but, at best, with pity for his beaten-up fur and lack of a prosperous rabbit hole. With each outing, the story became more and more removed from its original text. It became darker and the trials of the rabbit more unbearable. John's thoughts about it, however, were made abundantly clear. It was his commentary and lament that we, as a nation, forget too easily the sacrifices our soldiers make and that we show very little gratitude when they return home from the fields of war.

On the final day of the weekend, all the participants were in great spirits and ready to find their way through an area called the Labyrinth. This is a mountainous, rugged, and broken terrain with washes and ridges running in many directions. It is supremely challenging to map and compass your way through. The students were divided into groups, each deciding and planning their own route. Both teachers stepped back, giving the students the chance to make their own decisions. Occasionally, John would not interfere when his teammates orienteered themselves into the wrong direction. To arrive at camp in darkness was a welcome opportunity to practice night navigation. Eventually, all the participants reached their destination at Reevis Mountain School.

Azmith reflected on his Challenge experience in a journal entry to his wife during a marriage encounter weekend:

> The feeling I have that is most difficult to share is how to explain the joy I have had in working with young people when I know you feel uncomfortable with me being away from you and the family. Working with them has always given me the image of planting seeds or budding trees that will grow fruit in the future. The kidding and joking with young people keeps me close to youth—when I lose that connection, I see myself drifting away to Sun City. The trips replace the feeling of danger, adventure, and command that I miss from the army, which was so much a part of my formative years. Going on trips with adults, even with Bigfoot, does not pose the same kind of leadership challenge that whipping green, raw recruits into shape does, thus helping them to become confident, mature adults. Not to go with the students on outings would make me feel like a commander whose regiment went overseas without him.

In his historical files, John kept a treasured memento written by a group of Challenge graduates. They entitled their poem "Challenge Is":

- Reaching your goal no matter how impossible it may seem

- Speaking the truth and learning to see the truth in others

- Hitting the rapids and, at the end, finding you're the only one left in the boat

- Sharing your food no matter how little you have

- Making new friends and having them turn into old friends

- Wishing you were in a nice hot shower and standing in that nice hot shower and wishing you were still out hiking

- An opportunity to discover

- Living, learning, loving, and growing together as one big happy family

- Climbing a mountain to catch a falling star

- A group of people who can accept challenges of both the body and the mind, coming out of the experience a better, more complete person

- Wearing flowers, passing out T-shirts, climbing mountains, forming circles, holding hands, singing songs, giving back rubs

It is fitting to end this chapter on Challenge history with an abbreviated transcript of an e-mail from Barry Sweet, dated April 23, 2015:

We were kids. I am now an adult with a lifelong career as a Park Ranger in the National Park Service in Rocky Mountain National Park. My career is due largely to

John Goodson. He used the wilderness as a classroom and invited us through experiential education to learn outdoor skills and explore the wonders of the natural world. Whether it be exploring the Superstition Mountains or camping in the woods on the Mogollon Rim, we were alive—challenging the edge of our abilities and discovering the people we would become. And here I live now, years later, high up in the Rockies of Colorado protecting a world treasure with my life and preserving places of natural beauty. I think John Goodson would be proud.

The credit should go not only to John but also to all the advisers of the Challenge program who positively affected our students. We hear their stories, and we wish those stories to continue to inspire young people to find freedom from fear in their ongoing lives.

Reevis Mountain School

Peter was always curious to know why someone would be compelled to settle down and build hearth and home in a remote terrain. This was of particular interest to him when he backpacked through foreign lands.

Peter's opportunity to find out for himself came during a hike with a group of Challenge students in the Superstition Wilderness on Memorial Day 1978. Unexpectedly, they stumbled on a twelve-acre settlement located in a beautiful narrow valley. It was protected from further development as it was surrounded by national forest on three sides. The property was only accessible by a dead-end dirt road. Occasionally, that rough road became impassable during monsoon season.

All the buildings had been boarded up and were in a state of collapse. Without human interference, the land had turned into a playground for deer, foxes, raccoons, and mountain lions along with the usual assortment of small critters such as rattlesnakes, scorpions, brown recluse spiders, and crab spiders, which do bite people but at least are not poisonous, just painful.

Peter felt an instant recognition of this place and wanted to become its caretaker. He wanted it to be his site of operation, and he wanted to live there. The property that had touched Peter's heart and mind was a venerable Arizona territory. W. T. and A. Gaan were the couple who first saw the land's potential to be a self-sustaining ranch. But they decided to abandon it when their eighteen-month-old baby, Ida Mae, was stung by a scorpion. There is a memento marking their life at this place, a gravestone dated 1891.

The Gaan family left, and the Campaign property (as it was called in reference to Campaign Creek) changed ownership several times. Living there was not easy. The inhabitants had to grow all their own food, for example. After all, shopping for groceries required a two-day wagon trip to Globe.

By 1916, the property's title was transferred to Ed Horrell. Initially, it was used as a cattle roundup camp. In 1925, the land received a Homestead Act deed signed by Calvin Coolidge. When the Tonto National Forest was formed, the land was grandfathered in as a private inholding. Ed Horrell retained ownership until 1928, when he sold it to his son, Earl E. Horrell. Earl and his wife, Blanche, lived there until 1933. As others before them had done, they grew hay, grain, and vegetables. They also maintained an orchard and had pecan and walnut trees. In 1968, their daughter, Earlene, and her husband, Jim Tidwell—a local rancher and businessman—purchased the property.

One-hundred-year-old farmhouse at Reevis Ranch (Peter Busnack)

While restoring the old farmhouse, Peter discovered a quarter-inch piece of sheetrock with the date 1921 engraved on it. That is a good indication that the house is almost one hundred years old. None of its subsequent owners made any structural changes on the building until Peter replaced the wooden shingles with fireproof metal ones.

It was Peter's destiny and good fortune to find the property. He realized that attaining ownership of it, however, required the realities of dealing with business and finance. But he saw no problem in that. His good friend John could certainly find a solution. When these two comrades combined their creative energies on a "make the world better" project, the magic happened. In this case, they inspired a group of friends—ones who shared similar philosophies and practices of health and planetary responsibility—to form a partnership to buy the land. Its present owner, Jim Tidwell, had rejected many purchase offers over the years. But he approved of the partnership's plans, especially when Peter mentioned that the project included growing an organic vegetable garden and planting an orchard. This information by itself assuaged Tidwell's concerns, and he agreed to entrust his family's heritage from three generations to the group.

One of the Reevis Mountain School logos (Peter Busnack)

The investors called the endeavor "4E." The symbol stands for "ecological, environmental experiment for everyone." They planned to establish an educational entity focusing on self-sufficiency and outdoor survival skills. They gave it the official title of Reevis Mountain School. It is often referred to as just Reevis so it can not be confused with the Reavis Ranch apple orchard located in the vicinity.

Peter teaching at Reevis Mountain School (Peter Busnack)

Peter moved onto the property in 1980 and taught his first class there in that same year. One of the students, Lee Ann Aronson, recorded the following remembrance of her experience:

> Hearing Peter Bigfoot's survival story about his solo hike across the desert from New River to Four Peaks in the scorching heat of summer without taking any water, compelled me to sign up for the first class he taught at Reevis Mountain School in 1980. His message of self-reliant living in the Sonoran Desert was one that I wanted to experience. We learned so very much in the first class. There was knife-sharpening, how to build an adobe shelter, water-finding techniques, using a map and compass, the best wood to use to make a bow-and-drill to start a fire, finding food, making cordage for snares, repairing torn cloth with an agave "needle-and-thread," and so on.

Reevis Mountain School entrance sign (Peter Busnack)

Over the years, the school's program expanded to include meditation, Japanese fingertip acupuncture, native herbology, and stone masonry. The school also produces herbal remedies and a premiere, high-quality chaparral tea. John offered his land navigation course as an adjunct to the Reevis Mountain School curriculum. He engaged some of his friends to be instructors, including Glen Bobo, Paul Davis, and Sven Tonisson.

The Challenge program settled comfortably into a relationship with this new entity. Reevis was a good gateway into the Superstition Wilderness. Students also enjoyed hiking to the old apple orchard planted by Elisha M. Reavis, "the old hermit of the mountains." Even after the apple orchard was abandoned, some of the three hundred trees still produce apples in a good year. The location of this historic site is at 4,800 feet in elevation, about seven miles southwest of Reevis Mountain School.

The farm at Reevis Mountain School (Peter Busnack)

The day to day activities at Reevis include planting trees, growing vegetables, and protecting its chickens from wild beasts. It has been Peter's good fortune that, from the very beginning, the investors instituted an active internship program. These noble interns became Peter's volunteer brigade. As Peter had promised to Jim Tidwell there are once again a large vegetable garden and one hundred fruit trees. The names of the hardworking volunteers who helped Peter create this earthly paradise are not engraved in stone tablets as they should be, yet the contributions they made are significant and shall be forever remembered with gratitude.

Over the years, Reevis became Peter's permanent home and the Reevis Mountain School his life's work. Peter will say that, ultimately, Reevis civilized him. For John Goodson, Reevis was a lifelong source that sustained his spirit and kept him connected to the natural world he so relished as a young Kachina mountaineer.

Peter grinding roots on one-hundred-year-old equipment
(Peter Busnack, Reevis Archives)

The focus of Reevis Mountain School has mellowed over the years. Increasingly, the emphasis became herbology, the healing arts, and meditative practices. Even though it is not taught, the feeling of being in harmony with the trees, the plants and the stars abounds. What Reevis does teach is that the magic only happens after a day spent weeding the vegetable garden, gathering herbs in the desert, or distilling healing tinctures.

It should be noted that some time has passed since Peter last taught a class on desert survival—perhaps the time has come for a new generation of Kachina commandos to pick up and carry the banner.

PAAK Challenge and Reevis carried forth the legacy of the Kachinas, which is to educate people about ourselves and our planet. The character of the foundation is to offer to people of all ages a variety of indoor and outdoor educational experiences as is appropriate to accomplish this purpose.

In recent years, the PAAK Foundation has become an umbrella organization for several nonprofit institutions that share our goals. Tom Sonandres has kept the foundation intact for many years through its various transitions.

Acknowledgments

This book is the inspiration of Siglinde Goodson. After the death of her husband, John, she persuaded me to write it. We believe he would be proud of the result. In addition, Siglinde did a fine job of writing part 4.

The professional editors for the book were Leah Downing and Lisa Cerasoli. Thanks for your good work.

Sue Lefebvre, my wife, had her turn editing the text and preparing and placing the photographs. I value her many suggestions and personal support.

Thanks to the many alumni of the Kachinas, PAAK Challenge, and Reevis Mountain School programs whom I interviewed. Your memories of events were amazing, and your appreciation of those events was inspirational to me.

Printed in the United States
By Bookmasters